The Environment Comes Home

K. David Pijawka
Kim Shetter
with a Foreword by John Meunier

The Environment Comes Home

Arizona Public Service's Environmental Showcase Home

Contributors
Terry Hudgins
Brent Gifford
Mark Wilhelm
Tom Hahn
Edward Jones
Ron Mark
Willa Cree
Patricia Jones

Herberger Center for Design Excellence
College of Architecture and Environmental Design
Arizona State University

Herberger Center for Design Excellence
College of Architecture and Environmental Design
Arizona State University, Tempe, AZ 85287-1905

Alfred C. Sanft, Art Director
Piyada Kai Ekbundit, Graphic Designer
Cindy L. Thomas, Editorial Consultant
Sandy Batalden, Editorial Consultant

Book design by Alfred C. Sanft, Sanft Design Inc.
and Piyada Kai Ekbundit

Cover photograph and photographs on pages 18,
21, 22, 31, 39, 51, 58, 81, and 82 by Scot Zimmerman
Photograph on page 5 by John Schneeman
All other photographs by Howard Matt and Loren
Anderson of Arizona Public Service Company.
Computer graphics on pages 35, 78, and 96 by
Michael Clement, Arizona State University
Illustrative Subdivision Site Plan on page 101 by
Michael Underhill, Arizona State University

Distributed by:
The University of Arizona Press
1230 North Park Avenue, Suite 102
Tucson, AZ 85719
602-621-1441

ISBN 1-884320-13-9

Printed on Potlatch Corporation's Vintage Remar-
que Velvet, with 10 percent de-inked postconsumer
waste fiber and a total of 50 percent recycled fiber
(exceeds EPA guidelines for recycled paper)

Produced on Macintosh™ Quadra 800 using MS
Word 5.0®, QuarkXpress 3.3®, Adobe Illustrator 5.0®,
Adobe Photoshop 3.0®, and Aldus TrapWise 2.1®.

Printed by Arizona Public Service Printing Services
using a Two-color Heidelberg MOZP 19"x 25" press.

Inks: Four color process, Pantone® 116, Pantone®
465, Pantone® Reflex Blue, matte black, matte varnish, gloss varnish.

Those who worked to make the Environmental Showcase Home a reality did so in order to create a sustainable future for their children. We dedicate this book to their, and our, children.

Allison, Robin, Matthew, Kristen, Lindsey, Robert, Tobin, Diana, Alexandra, Chelsea Faith, Andrea, Nicole, Michelle, Monica, Gretchen, Frank, Donna, Leah, Lacy, Richard, Jeanette, Kristin, Anthony, Michele, Marcia, Miranda, Michael, Melissa, Angela, Tamara, Danae, Robert, James, Rebecca, Jonathan, Jennifer, Stephanie, Nicholas, Stacy Lee, Rhianna, Ryan, Erin, Shelley, Stacey, McKay, Andrew, Kyle, Elyse, Padraic, Colin, Justin, Daniel, Christina, Benjamin, Sarah, and Drew.

Environmental Advisory Committee

Laura M. Watson, Chair	Desert House
Jack Bale	Arizona Department of Environmental Quality
Dan Campbell	Arizona Chapter Nature Conservancy
Lauren Evans	Arizona Department of Environmental Quality
Fred Fleet	Ducks Unlimited
Sheila Grinell	Arizona Museum of Science and Technology
Jack Haenichen	Arizona Department of Commerce, Energy Office
Barbara Louise Hill	United States Environmental Protection Agency
Frederick S. Leif	United States Environmental Protection Agency
Sue Lofgren	Community Volunteer
Karen O'Regan	City of Phoenix, Office of Environmental Programs
K. David Pijawka	Arizona State University
Barbara Spark	United States Environmental Protection Agency
Don Steuter	Conservation Committee, Sierra Club
Roger Tomalty	Arcosanti

Arizona Environmental Strategic Alliance

John Wise	United States Environmental Protection Agency
Frederick S. Leif	United States Environmental Protection Agency
Barbara Louise Hill	United States Environmental Protection Agency
Jack Bale	Arizona Department of Environmental Quality
Lauren Evans	Arizona Department of Environmental Quality
Edward Z. Fox	Arizona Department of Environmental Quality
William D. Wiley	Arizona Department of Environmental Qualtiy
Beverly Westgaard	Arizona Department of Environmental Quality
Bob Munari	Arizona Department of Environmental Quality
Terry Hudgins	Arizona Public Service
Janie Holmes	Arizona Public Service

General Contractor

Fred Homes	Homes & Son Contractors, Inc.
Robert Levenda	Homes & Son Contractors, Inc.
Brian Kleve	Homes & Son Contractors, Inc.

Arizona Public Service

Brent Gifford
J. F. Castillo
Steve Dalton
Mark Wilhelm
Sally Stewart Haines
Jo Lou Spleth

Boyd Titus
Howard Matt
William Pascarella
Timothy Mahoney
Terry Ricketts
Herb Hacker

Judy Swartz
Richard MacLean
Phil Saladino
Cynthia Slick
John Duncan
Vernon J. Dail

Terry Hudgins
Robert McLellan
Janie Holmes
Annette King
Donald Happ
Danielle Luko

Architectural and Engineering Team

Edward Jones — Jones Studio, Inc.
Neal Jones — Jones Studio, Inc.
Tom Hahn — Jones Studio, Inc.
Ron Mark — Xeris Group
Robert Thompson — Richard Emik Associates, Inc.
Ray McNulty — McNulty and Associates, Inc.
Roger Smith — Lighting Dynamics, Inc.
Rob Meade — Grommes-Meade Engineering, Inc.
Mel Slaysman — Slaysman Engineering, Inc.
Dave Nykorchuk — DNA Engineering, Inc.
Pamela Barnes — Allegro Business Interiors
Carmen Tenney — Allegro Business Interiors

Independent Advisors

Bob Boscamp — EcoGroup, Inc.
Steve Loken — Center for Resourceful Building Technology
Connie Wilhelm — Home Builders Association of Central Arizona
Amory Lovins — Rocky Mountain Institute
Jeff Shively — Arizona Department of Commerce, Energy Office
Charles Gohman — Arizona Department of Commerce, Energy Office
Charles Sherman — Energy Simulation Specialists
David Tait — Tait Solar Company
David Scheatzle — Arizona State University
Martin Pasqualetti — Arizona State University
John Meunier — Arizona State University

Contents

1. From Idea to Design

2. Energy Efficiency

List of Tables and Figures

Foreword

John Meunier
Dean, College of Architecture and Environmental Design
Arizona State University

Until the widespread use of electrically powered central air conditioning, the Sonoran Desert had been a peculiarly demanding place in which to build a home for year-round living. Summer days, when the temperature can exceed 100 degrees Fahrenheit for more than three months of the year, caused earlier builders to think hard about issues such as shade, orientation, cross-ventilation, planting around the home, and the desirability of verandahs, sleeping porches, shaded patios, and indoor/outdoor rooms such as the "Arizona Room." They developed building forms that responded in varying ways to their circumstances.

The Anasazi, the Sinagua, the Hohokam, indeed all the indigenous peoples, developed ways of building which offered deep shade in the summer and access to the benevolent sun in the winter. The early Hispanic settlers from Spain and Mexico brought with them cool shady courtyards with fruit trees and fountains. The early Anglo settlers, arriving without a tradition of central courtyards, nonetheless surrounded their buildings with deep porches that not only shaded the interiors but provided protected outdoor living spaces. The ranch house developed in response to the climate and became a durable type: typically a simple rectangle with its long sides oriented to the north and the south, with a porch on the easily shaded south side where the high summer sun was much more controllable than the low eastern and western sun of the morning and evening.

The Environmental Showcase Home, sponsored, ironically, by a power company whose electricity drives the air conditioning that has all but destroyed the above traditions, clearly reestablishes those same traditions. But it does so not in a self-conscious historically revivalist way. This is not the false pueblo style which pervades Santa Fe with its contemporary rusticity. This is a carefully researched, technologically up-to-date, rationally ordered building, which takes full advantage of recent developments in our understanding of what it means to be environmentally conscious. That it turns out to be within the tradition of the ranch house implies no more than that the forces of nature in the Sonoran Desert have not changed, and that our forebears had, perforce, to be intelligent in confronting them.

It gives me a peculiar pleasure to recognize these ironies: that a power company should find it appropriate to show us how to save electricity, and that a modern architect, with all the commitment to radical thinking that that implies, should find himself designing within a tradition long predating the modern era. But it gives me very particular satisfaction to think that, with this house, we may be returning to the question of what is an appropriate "Phoenix Style," not just of building form but also of a way of life.

This house is not just a "shopping center" of technological concepts and products that can lessen our burden on the environment. That is, in itself, a profoundly worthy enterprise: learning to "reduce, reuse, and recycle" when we build our homes makes both ethical and economic sense, allowing us to build without destroying our ecological heritage for future generations. Beyond its technology, however, the design of this home also shows us how to live our day-to-day domestic lives in greater harmony with the daily and annual rhythms of our extraordinary setting, the Sonoran Desert.

Eddie Jones, the architect of the home, belongs to what some call the organic school of architectural theory. Frank Lloyd Wright, the most powerful spokesman for organic architecture, spent many years living and working in the Arizona desert. In a 1940 article for *Arizona Highways*, he recorded his ideas about how architecture should adapt itself to this unique environment. A reliance on forms and structures from other climates was not, in his eyes, a valid response to the desert:

The Arizona desert is no place for the hard box walls of the houses of the Middle West and East. Here all is sculptured by wind and water, patterned in color and texture. A desert building should be nobly simple in outline as the region itself is sculptured: should have learned from the cactus many secrets of straight-line patterns for its forms, playing with the light and softening the building into its proper place among the organic desert creations— the man-made building heightening the beauty of the desert and the desert more beautiful because of the building. A dream, but realization is coming.

Some would say that Wright was too optimistic, but others might recognize that in this Environmental Showcase Home some, at least, of those ideals are being ful- filled. It is worthy of your attention.

Acknowledgments

In the course of writing this book, we received support and assistance from many individuals and organizations who were involved in the planning, design, and building of the Environmental Showcase Home (ESH). A grant from Arizona Public Service (APS) to Arizona State University's (ASU) College of Architecture and Environmental Design and to the Herberger Center for Design Excellence made this book possible. APS made available to us all their meeting notes, files, plans, and records regarding the home and gave us complete independence in its evaluation.

Several professionals provided us with valuable insights into various aspects of the home. Energy Simulation Specialists in Tempe, Arizona, conducted energy simulation analyses for the ESH that show the energy use outcomes of the appliances and energy systems in the home. Tom Hines of EcoGroup Inc. researched the energy implications of water savings. Martin Pasqualetti, a geographer at ASU, provided us with analytical data on the environmental benefits of the home's reduction in energy use. Michael Underhill, Director of ASU's School of Architecture, shared with us his plans for subdivision development using various housing densities based on ESH designs and principles. The contributions made by these individuals added significantly to the book.

John Meunier, Dean of ASU's College of Architecture and Environmental Design, wrote the foreword that places the ESH in its context of southwestern architectural history, the Sonoran Desert environment, and sustainable design philosophy. Meunier's commitment to the educational value of the home and the advancement of architectural quality in the community is reflected in his involvement as a juror in the ESH competition, an advisor to APS, and the host of a television series featuring the home.

We are grateful to Terry Hudgins, the person behind the book at APS. Understanding that a document for the public would be the best way to communicate the experience APS had gained from building the home, he coordinated the effort at APS. He gave us plans, documents, advisory reports, and construction specifications; reviewed our draft chapters; held our hands at the most difficult times; and never faltered from the original goal.

Other APS reviewers, including Richard MacLean, William Pascarella, Mark Wilhelm, John Duncan, and Rebecca Watral, provided clarification of many technical and historical matters. We owe a special thanks to Howard Matt of APS who went out of his way to provide us with the photographs we needed for the book.

Steve Loken and Tracy Mumma of the Center for Resourceful Building Technology gave us thoughtful comments on chapter 4. We are grateful to them for their time and for sharing with us their knowledge of environmental building materials.

Many individuals contributed to the book directly. We thank Richard MacLean, Terry Hudgins, Frederick Steiner, Steve Loken, Martin Pasqualleti and John Wise for writing the sidebars that contribute their unique perspectives on sustainable design and environmental homebuilding. We also interviewed many of the principals involved in the project, including Mark DeMichele, Edward Jones, Tom Hahn, Mark Wilhelm, Robert Thompson, Ron Mark, Fred Homes, and Ray McNulty. They generously shared their time and expertise with us.

We are especially grateful to our colleagues at Arizona State University who reviewed individual chapters or the entire manuscript. Professors Joseph Ewan, Edward Cook, Ruth Yabes, and Subhrajit Guhathakurta were excellent reviewers and added much to the quality and completeness of the book. Professor Duncan Patten, ecologist, reviewed the entire manuscript; his questions and comments were especially helpful in our revisions. As he is building his own environmental home in Montana, we spent many hours at the Center for Environmental Studies sharing information and discussing issues of environmental home design. The book has been enriched through his involvement.

The Herberger Center for Design Excellence, directed by Beverly Brandt, and the School of Planning and Landscape Architecture, under the leadership of Frederick Steiner, provided the support we needed to undertake this book project. Willa Cree and Patricia Jones contributed a great deal of research to this project, providing background information on environmental and energy issues, other green homes in the United States and Canada, and materials used in the ESH.

Brent Gifford probably knows the ESH better than anyone else. As the home's project manager, it was his responsibility to take it from concept to reality. He never once failed to respond to our questions and requests for design plans, photographs, descriptions of materials and features, tours of the home, and analyses of its systems. The ESH and the book could not have been completed without his tireless efforts, knowledge, and enthusiastic support.

Edward Jones of Jones Studio, Inc., the principal architect of the ESH, gave much of his time to help us understand how his art, philosophies, and commitment to environmental design went into this home. Architect Tom Hahn of Jones Studio, who researched the building materials that were used, has become a national expert on environmentally responsible building materials. We appreciate the preliminary draft he wrote of chapter 4, his detailed review of the draft manuscript, and the contribution he made to the accuracy of our research.

Piyada Kai Ekbundit created the book and cover design under the direction of Al Sanft, of Sanft Design Inc. The striking computer graphics of the home were developed by Michael Clements and generously donated to the book by APS. Bob McLellan, manager of APS's print shop, worked with us to make sure we would have a book of the finest quality. We owe a particular debt of gratitude to Cindy Thomas, whose editing skills were put to the test at every stage of this project.

Our sincere thanks to the individuals mentioned above, without whose help this book would not have been possible.

Preface

After two years of planning and design and eight months of construction, the Arizona Public Service (APS) Environmental Showcase Home is a reality. Using the latest design, technology, and materials, its architects and builders have created a structure that points the way to a sustainable future. We have learned much from the project—now we invite the community of homebuilders and home buyers to share in our findings and carry those efforts forward.

This book documents the ideas, strategies, design, and construction of the APS Environmental Showcase Home. The project would not have been completed without a team of dedicated and committed professionals at APS, the U.S. Environmental Protection Agency (EPA), the Arizona Department of Environmental Quality (ADEQ), the Home Builders Association of Central Arizona, the Arizona Department of Commerce Energy Office, as well as representatives of environmental organizations, government agencies, and homebuilders who served on various advisory committees. APS is proud to be a part of the search for better energy efficiency, more effective materials reuse, improved water conservation techniques, and design for sustainability—issues that will carry over into the next century.

Why did we do it? Why would a utility company, whose primary mandate is to provide energy to its customers, branch out into the field of homebuilding? In these introductory pages, I would like to explain the philosophy and motivation behind the APS Environmental Showcase Home.

When I came to APS in 1978, part of my vision for the state's largest electric utility was that it should participate fully in its community. I felt that the role of a utility company should be larger than just a supplier of energy to its customers. It should work with them as an equal partner to discover the best solutions to energy-related problems—problems such as the special need for energy efficiency, waste reduction, and resource conservation in our Southwestern desert environment.

About four years ago, I began a dialogue with Bill Reilly, who was the administrator of the EPA at the time. We talked at length about how a corporation could be involved in environmental programs in a way that would make a significant difference in its community. APS's relationship with the EPA evolved into the Arizona Environmental Strategic Alliance, which ultimately included the ADEQ.

It was my desire to address the larger need for fundamental change in how we live in the Phoenix metropolitan area. We live in the desert—an environmentally fragile area. We depend heavily on energy for our lifestyle and comfort. Our water comes from distant sources—flowing hundreds of miles through canals that cross the arid desert. At APS, we asked ourselves how we could expand our educational efforts to include these broader issues.

The APS Environmental Showcase Home is a shopping center of environmentally responsible products, architectural concepts, environmental strategies, and a central body of knowledge at one location. Our intent was to increase awareness and to influence those who impact the construction of entire subdivisions, not just individual homes—the construction industry and its allies. At the same time, the home offers an opportunity for members of the public to learn how their home-buying habits can have a significant impact on our natural resources, as well as on energy and water bills.

Until now, the most common type of home available in Arizona has been a California-style home that has been transplanted to the desert. In this energy-conscious age, it is obvious that the oversized windows and high ceilings of this type of home are not an efficient way to cope with the desert climate. As we considered the idea of a change in home design that would result in the conservation of energy, other conservation issues became apparent.

There is no doubt in my mind that water, which has until now been cheap and plentiful in our area, will become an expensive commodity in the coming years.

As the former chairman of the Governor's Committee on the Central Arizona Project, I can see that there will be no choice but to raise water prices steadily through the end of this decade, and water conservation will become a high priority in the Phoenix area. In addition to the water issue, the problem of municipal waste disposal is an important one, both now and in the future. It will become more and more important to use construction materials that are either environmentally compatible or made of recycled goods.

The above conservation issues led us to commit over two years' worth of time and resources to research, design, and construct the Environmental Showcase Home. With its completion, we hope to push the market into understanding and accepting the concepts the home demonstrates. If the public embraces the ideas of the home design, it will create a demand in the Phoenix market for similar energy-efficient and resource-conserving buildings.

The public will do this only if the home is attractive and livable. We have avoided the pitfalls of other environmental homes by creating a light and airy interior space and extending the living areas to the outdoors. These features, along with many other design amenities, bring market acceptability to the home.

As the design work proceeded on the home and we realized its potential for reducing energy consumption, enhancing water conservation, and ensuring resource efficiency in materials selection, we became more aware of the substantial indirect environmental benefits that result from environmentally responsible building. For instance, air emissions—a by-product of the generation of electricity—could be substantially lowered as we reduce our consumption of and demand for electricity.

Financial considerations should also make this home attractive to the buyer. One of the benefits of purchasing a home as energy efficient as this one (60 percent more energy efficient than the typical Phoenix production home without using solar technologies) is that most people would be able to qualify for a higher mortgage than they might normally seek. If they save money on their energy bill and on their water bill, they can apply that money to a mortgage payment. This advantage gives the buyer greater flexibility in negotiations with the bank.

Our hope for this project, with its emphasis on conservation and education, is that it will become a key example of environmentally concerned design for the Southwestern desert region of Arizona. The comfort and beauty of this home are not just in its outward appearance, but in the principles of sustainability, energy efficiency, and resource efficiency that it embodies. It is tangible evidence of the idea that a utility must be a good steward not only of its own business, but also of its community.

Mark DeMichele
President and Chief Executive Officer
Arizona Public Service Company

Mark DeMichele makes decision to build an environmental home

Arizona Environmental Strategic Alliance is formed with EPA

Focus group research is completed

Design Work Group reports are filed

Design Issues Guide is completed

1992

| Jan 92 | Apr | Jul | Oct | Nov | Dec | Jan 93 | Feb |

19

Initial draft of marketing plan is presented

APS sends out request for qualifications and rules for architect selection competition

Architectural competition is held, and Jones Studio is chosen as architect. Work is begun on developing design concepts presented in competition

Initial APS project team is formed: project kickoff

APS completes
purchase of lot

Public participation
meetings are held in
neighborhood

Jones Studio com-
pletes final design

Environmental
Advisory Committee
starts to meet

Completion
of home

ADEQ joins
Strategic Alliance

Sitework begins

1994

Jun   Jul   Aug   Nov   Dec   Jan 94 Feb   Apr   Oct   Nov   Dec   Jan 95

23

Jones Studio pre-
sents first complete
design

Design is reviewed
by various industry
and target audience
groups

Final draft of
marketing plan is
completed

Grand
opening
of Environ-
mental
Showcase
Home

Construction kickoff

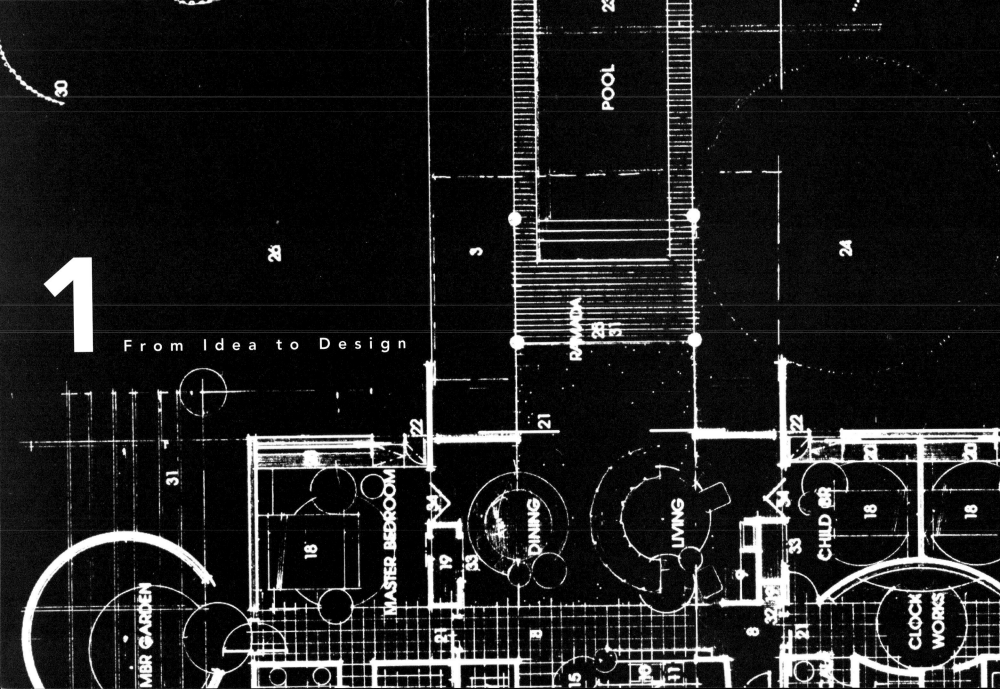

1

From Idea to Design

Arizona Public Service Company (APS), Arizona's largest electric utility company, has built a home designed to cut down on our use of natural resources. With a combination of energy-efficient technology and environmentally sensitive design, the Environmental Showcase Home (ESH) saves energy, water, and materials, creating a new standard for sustainable building in the Southwest desert. It highlights the connection, not always apparent, between the homes we live in and our environment—a connection that needs to be made explicit with every new home we build.

In addition to saving energy, water, and materials, the home is designed to create less pollution than a standard production home does, from the manufacture of the construction materials to the final walk-through and beyond. It is designed to accomplish these goals without deviating from a practical, affordable, buildable ideal that can be attained by any homebuilder or home buyer using today's materials and technology. In short, this home is intended to satisfy the concerns of today's environmental community without sacrificing the basic pragmatic precepts of those who build, live in, and eventually pay for the greatest investment that a typical homeowner will make.

The ESH is located in the northeast part of the city of Phoenix, on a residential lot in a recently developed subdivision. It calls attention to itself subtly because it has none of the hallmarks of

Opposite page: Blueprint of ESH floor plan by Jones Studio, Inc.

Phoenix, Arizona

recent subdivision architecture: it has no red tile roof, no windows that face the summer sun, no expanse of green lawn, no "Spanish-style" arches spanning its concrete driveway, and, in fact, no concrete driveway. It rests comfortably in its surroundings, its elements working with nature rather than defying it.

What the home does have is the latest environmental designs and technologies that are transferable, right now, to any new home or subdivision project in the area. A builder of new homes can make use of many of the materials and techniques on display in this home: there is nothing experimental or unavailable that would discourage a builder from accepting the ideas of the home. An owner of an existing home can also use the ideas of the ESH to retrofit an older home with the latest energy- and water-saving technologies.

This is a showcase home. It was built to show all of us what can be done in the area of residential construction that can help us cut down on our use of water and energy. Although the home's creation was anything but simple, in its finished state it addresses with simplicity some of our most pressing environmental problems.

The designers and builders of the ESH intended that its ideas should be applicable to all homebuilding in our desert environment. Environmental homes in other parts of the country must respond to other regional climates, resulting in appearances and functions suited to their areas. Similarly, the ESH has designs, technologies, and materials suited to the Southwest desert and dictated by the almost constant presence of the desert sun. Windows are placed to avoid its heat, while water heaters and photovoltaic cells are placed to absorb it. The shape and siting of the home, the layout of the interior space, the design of the landscape—all are governed by the direction and seasonal intensity of sunlight. The ESH looks and functions the way it does because of where it was built.

If the home is successful, and on many levels it is, then the materials and methods used in its construction could set a course for future building. The construction of the home will inspire those who are serious about preserving our Southwest desert to learn about and understand the impact that our dwelling places and building practices have on the environment. No longer can we

afford to be wasteful with our natural resources, and the dwellings we choose to inhabit must be among the first things we change if we are to attain a sustainable future in the desert.

Home Construction in the Desert

Phoenix is located in the Sonoran Desert of central Arizona, one of the hottest and driest climates in the Southwest. The climate of Phoenix and the surrounding metropolitan area, known as the Valley of the Sun, has long attracted people from other parts of the country, especially since the widespread adoption of air conditioning in the 1950s has mitigated the hot summers. Arizona's average annual population growth rate is approximately 2.5 percent, with the new residents creating a demand for new home construction. In 1993, over 22,000 building permits were issued in the greater Phoenix area, a 23 percent increase over 1992, just missing a 1986 record.

The typical production home in Phoenix is built to be cost-effective rather than environmentally efficient. The desert climate is ideal for solar energy application, yet little solar use is discernible throughout the area. Water is a precious resource, yet the Phoenix area has not adopted drought-resistant landscaping in any meaningful way. Partly because of financial pressures and the perceived unavailability of environmentally responsible materials, but mostly because of the lack of knowledge on the part of the public, there has been virtually no market demand for homes that fulfill an environmentally conscious ideal.

In the present homebuilding climate, there is little public mandate for environmentally efficient homes: builders do not want to build homes for which there is no public demand, buyers are unaware of the impact of their home-buying choices, lenders are reluctant to fund anything new and unproven, and regulatory agencies do not have the power to create demand for such products. During a 1992 focus group of local home buyers, researchers contracted by APS were surprised to find out that "the participants need to have explained *how using less energy is better for the environment*" (their italics). The researchers concluded that members of the public do not normally associate environmental issues with the kinds of homes they purchase.

The public's lack of knowledge can be characterized in two ways. First, as demonstrated by the focus group, most people do not realize how the homes they buy affect the environment. Many people who carpool, recycle their newspapers, and send money to environmental groups have typically not considered how the home they choose to live in affects the environment they are trying to save. Second, if they do become aware of the connection between the environment and home design and construction techniques, they do not know how to address their concerns in an effective manner. APS hopes to be able to bridge this gap between intent and action by showing what can be done with materials and techniques available now to the average homebuilder.

There have been some building programs in the Valley that have encouraged the construction of energy-saving homes. Three production builder programs, each administered by a different local utility, are the Climate Crafted Program by the Salt River Project, the Energy Advantage Program by Southwest Gas Company, and the Good

The Arizona desert

An Agenda for Change

Resource-efficient construction is cost-effective only insofar as the designer/ builder is determined to "find a better way." Projects like the ESH provide the means for a dialogue on the subject and bring together otherwise disparate groups to discuss the issues and offer a forum for these products. The inertia of designers and builders may ultimately get the cooperation of government agencies. Once agencies become comfortable with these new ideas, methods, and products and revise their codes to reflect that understanding, the large-scale changes we all hope for will be much more rapid.

(From an article by Tom Hahn of Jones Studio in the Spring 1994 issue of *Recycling Review*)

Cents Home Program by Arizona Public Service. APS introduced the Good Cents Home Program to help builders meet the energy-efficiency requirements of the federal government. With the construction of the ESH, APS hopes to take the involvement of a public utility in homebuilding to a new level.

Becoming an Environmental Leader

APS provides electric service in nearly 250 communities in Arizona, reaching approximately 45 percent of Arizona's population. APS's generating facilities have a capacity of over four million kilowatts; the main fuel sources for those facilities include nuclear power (Palo Verde Nuclear Generating Facility) and coal (Four Corners, Navajo, and Cholla).

Certain APS officials have long realized the unique influence a utility company can have on environmental issues. As early as 1973, APS created an environmental department in order to establish environmental policies that could guide its business practices.

In 1988, after having served ten years in other capacities, Mark DeMichele became president and chief executive officer of the company. With his personal commitment to environmental issues, he has been involved for many years in the national and international debate over electric industries and their effect on the environment. He chairs the Edison Electric Institute's Global Warming Task Force and has participated in numerous national, state, and local committees that set new environmental policies and programs. Under his leadership, APS has increased its environmental activities, and was the first electric utility in the nation to endorse the Clean Air Act Amendments in 1990.

DeMichele and other company officials were already aware that "environmentalism" had become a core value of society. Their own 1991 survey had established that 72 percent of APS's customers labeled themselves "environmentalists" or "conservationists." For many reasons, APS officials wanted to reflect their customers' environmental values in the programs of the company, including the ESH project. The average person has poorly understood the connection of homebuilding to environmental values—APS wanted to make that connection visible.

Another reason for the company's involvement with environmental home construction is purely economic. If its customers demand less energy, then APS can delay the construction of future power-generating plants. It is estimated that the 12,000 new Phoenix-area homes added to the APS power grid in 1993 require 40 megawatts at peak demand. If these homes had been built to be more energy-efficient, then 4 megawatts of coincident peak demand could have been shaved from summer peak growth. Any energy savings that APS can realize in the future will translate into less capital investment.

The idea of building a home to demonstrate environmental principles came from discussions in January 1992 between DeMichele and Richard MacLean, APS Vice President of Environmental Health and Safety. Their discussions led to the initiation of business practices that incorporated concepts of sustainable development, total environmental quality management, life cycle assessment, and pollution prevention into the day-to-day business operations of the company. They determined that the best way to demonstrate a sustainable future to the public was by building an environmentally responsible home in Phoenix.

You and I might drive by a typical new subdivision in Phoenix and see a pleasant landscape of lawns and spacious homes. DeMichele sees glass—large expanses of glass with an R-value rating of near zero, allowing heat to either penetrate (in the summer) or escape (in the winter) the interior of the home. He also sees grass—acres of well-tended Bermuda or rye grass, requiring an amount of water equal to 50 to 60 percent of the home's total water consumption. And he sees pavement—thousands of square feet of dense material forming a heat sink that radiates the summer day's high temperatures back out into the night, creating what scientists call the "heat island effect" in Southwestern urban areas. Underground there are pipes that bring water over hundreds of miles of desert to irrigate the landscape, pipes that carry used water away, and cables that bring electricity from west of Phoenix and from the Four Corners area to power air conditioners, water heaters, washers, dryers, refrigerators, and microwave ovens, most of which are not as energy-efficient as they can be.

DeMichele saw a great opportunity for reform in this water- and energy-consuming landscape. He believed that if his company could demonstrate a better way to live in the desert, a way that would save people money and would recapture the hidden environmental costs of the misuse of energy, water, and other resources, the long-term results would benefit both current and future residents of the Valley. In January 1992, officials at APS decided to build a residential home showcasing the latest environmental design and materials.

One of the first actions of company officials was to hire Brent Gifford as project manager in April 1992. He directed the operations for the three years it took to bring the ESH from conceptualization to completion.

The Strategic Alliance

In October 1992, eight months after the showcase home project was conceived, APS announced it had joined Region IX of the United States Environmental Protection Agency (EPA) to form the Arizona Environmental Strategic Alliance. The Arizona Department of Environmental Quality (ADEQ) joined the alliance in August 1993. The alliance was the first environmental partnership in the country that combined the resources of private industry and federal and state regulatory agencies for the purpose of environmental stewardship. Previously, relationships between business and its regulators had focused almost exclusively on compliance, but in this case the parties have agreed that collaborative environmental programs will be addressed separately from issues of compliance. The alliance allows the three partners to combine their talents and resources to achieve common goals, including environmental education, commitment to community, and pollution prevention.

Together, the members of the alliance have targeted five project areas in the state, including chlorofluorocarbon (CFC) reduction, environmental education for grades K–12, residential opportunities for environmental education, pollution prevention for small business owners, and the ESH. Though APS initiated the idea of the home before the alliance was formed, the home has become an important part of the alliance's goals and objectives.

Environmental Objectives

- Use materials that have verifiable environmental benefits as demonstrated by a life cycle or embodied-energy cost analysis.
- Reduce total indoor water use by more than 50 percent as compared to use in average existing homes.
- Reduce indoor air pollution (including particulates, molds, spores, formaldehyde, and carbon monoxide) as compared to that in standard electric and dual-fuel homes.
- Reduce total home construction waste production by 50 percent as compared to that produced during construction of an average home today.
- Reduce projected total waste stream during occupation of home by 50 percent.
- Build with significant amounts of recycled and otherwise resource-efficient building materials.
- Improve the demand for recycled building materials.
- Demonstrate environmentally sensitive pest control and deterrent systems.
- Demonstrate xeriscape technology for low-water consumption and microclimate improvement.
- Demonstrate land-use planning and development techniques that foster conservation.

Energy Efficiency Objectives

- Reduce total annual energy consumption by 50 percent as compared to a typical new energy-efficient home.
- Reduce coincident peak demand by 50 percent as compared to a typical new energy-efficient home.
- Increase total annual load factor by 20 percent as compared to a typical new energy-efficient home.
- Reduce annual energy bill by 30 percent as compared to a typical new energy-efficient home.
- Minimize the need for electric lighting during daylight hours.

Homebuilding Objectives

- Improve the energy efficiency of new production homes built within the metropolitan Phoenix region by an average of 10 percent within the next five years.
- See at least five of the home's energy-efficient strategies, components, or technologies adopted by at least three of the top twenty production builders as standard or as options within the next five years.
- See at least five of the home's environmentally sensitive strategies, components, or technologies adopted into use by at least three top production builders as standard or as options within the next five years.

1. APS objectives
for the environmental
home project

Development of a Marketing Plan

The technical issues of the project were clear to APS officials from the start: to build a home that would demonstrate various available methods and technologies that would lessen our use of energy, water, and materials. But a demonstration is effective only if it has an audience, and the officials first had to identify that audience.

Research by the marketing department led them to a target audience of five groups: production and custom builders, financial lenders, environmental leaders, the media, and the home-buying public. Of these groups, the two most important are homebuilders and home buyers, who together could create a new market for environmentally responsible homebuilding.

To the homebuilder, APS officials had to convey their environmental message without undue pressure or criticism. They understood that builders do a good job building homes that are cost-effective—what APS wanted builders to do was add environmental responsibility to their list of selling points for marketing. Production builders, a group of seventy-eight developers who are

responsible for about 90 percent of all the new, single-family homes each year in the Valley, were targeted as the major audience. Custom builders, though they are responsible for only 10 percent of the new home starts in the Valley, were seen as almost equally important because they are frequently the first to build with new technologies and are strongly influenced by consumer demand. To the home buyer, APS officials wanted to convey the message that ideals of environmental responsibility can be implemented when purchasing a new home. It was important to be clear about the home's objectives in order to appeal to these two groups of the proposed target audience.

In 1992, APS officials completed the ESH marketing plan, in which they articulated the home's goals and strategies. Three sets of objectives, listed in Table 1, gave the company a defined list of criteria by which to judge the final result. With input from other departments at APS, the marketing department classified the construction and building elements of the home into three groups: strategies, components, and technologies. For instance, a strategy might be a design element such as the orientation

of the home, a component might be a recycled material used in construction, and a technology might be a new energy-efficient air-handling system. This classification of elements served to organize and coordinate the work of many departments within APS and outside consultants throughout the building process. To further ensure that the objectives would be met, the project team wrote a definition of the home to serve as a standard for everyone who would eventually work on the project:

The APS Environmental Showcase Home will be a showcase of emerging housing technologies. It will demonstrate what can be done to reduce the impact of housing on the environment. Energy efficiency and environmental responsibility (water conservation, reduced pollution, use of recycled materials) will be critical elements of this home. The technologies to be demonstrated must be practical alternatives— either now or within the next two years— to present home construction standards.

APS's ultimate goal for the proposed environmental demonstration home is nothing less than to bring about a complete change in the home-buying

A Challenge for Builders

The challenge of building in more environmentally sensitive ways requires a mind open to new ideas and an ability and desire to understand new methods and materials. As resource extraction and consumption continue to become environmentally damaging and economically costly, sound alternatives will increasingly be in demand. Those builders who adapt and grow with the changes will certainly ensure the sustainability of the global resource base, the stability of the regional environment, and the security of their own livelihood.

(From Design Issues Guide, created for APS by EcoGroup, Inc. and the Center for Resourceful Building Technology)

preferences of the public. The marketing plan makes this clear:

> The Environmental Showcase Home is an education and demonstration project that is intended to move the new residential marketplace to one in which more energy-efficient and environmentally sensitive homes are built. This mission will be accomplished through the education of consumers, homebuilders and trade allies about the merits of building and purchasing energy-efficient and environmentally sensitive homes. To support this education effort, the home will serve as a site to demonstrate technologies, designer strategies, and building practices which lead to that end . . . . It is expected that this effort [together with other APS programs] . . . will make undeniable progress toward a new home marketplace in which more energy-efficient and environmentally sensitive homes will be built.

APS officials did not initiate and realize the ESH project in order to test specific products, or to experiment with new designs and technologies, or to provide an interesting educational experience for the visitor. Their goal was both broader and more farsighted:

it was to demonstrate the possibilities of environmentally responsible home-building with such emphasis that the target audience would respond by bringing about a shift in the marketplace to a new way of building.

Understanding Environmental Homes

APS's staff used several sources of information in the development of the project. To understand how the public might react to the ESH, they asked Westgroup Marketing Research in Phoenix to coordinate a series of focus groups in the fall of 1992. Westgroup researchers interviewed seven groups that would influence or be influenced by the development of the home: custom homebuilders, production home-builders, new or prospective home buyers, trade allies, appraisers, mortgage lenders, and environmentalists.

The purpose of the interviews was to get direct input from various target groups regarding the factors that should be considered in developing the ESH. The focus groups led the researchers to three conclusions.

First, they thought that the ESH was a logical starting point to begin an education process. If the public did not understand the connection between saving energy and the environment, as was demonstrated during the discussions, a well-designed environmental home might demonstrate the principles of energy conservation in ways that would be directly understandable. Second, most participants were interested in how such a home would save them money. Third, there was a certain amount of skepticism about APS's motives for becoming environmentally sensitive. Westgroup thought that APS should carefully explain its reasons for wanting to save energy so that people would understand the company's involvement in the ESH project.

The members of each focus group, though they supported the idea of saving energy and helping the environment, felt that their own particular group was not the one that was responsible for making any changes. All the groups looked to someone else to take the leadership role. Westgroup concluded that APS was a natural choice to fill that role, if it could successfully communicate its ideals to the public.

Though the focus groups gave APS insight into the human side of environmentally sensitive homes, the project team also needed to understand the technical side of green homes. For this information they first went to what Brent Gifford, APS's project manager for the ESH, calls the "best single resource nationwide" for information about environmental building materials, *GREBE*, the *Guide to Resource Efficient Building Elements*. Compiled by Steve Loken of the Center for Resourceful Building Technology (CRBT) in Missoula, Montana, it lists commercially available homebuilding materials that have minimum impacts on the environment. *GREBE* includes the pros and cons of various materials that are marketed for their environmental efficiency, including foundation materials, framing materials, siding, trim, and roofing material, carpet padding, and insulation. Loken chose products for *GREBE* because they were made from recycled components, were composed of easily renewable resources, or represented low-energy production methods.

APS hired CRBT and EcoGroup to create a design guide for the ESH. CRBT, based in Montana, is a nonprofit agency that was founded by Loken in 1990 to educate the public about environmental building materials and technologies that are available for home construction. Ecogroup is a local company that specializes in educating the public about the link between energy use and the environment. It has developed educational materials to demonstrate that the improvement of the environment is a direct result of how we conserve energy and resources. Together, experts from the two companies wrote the *Design Issues Guide* for the ESH in February 1993. The *Guide* recommends materials, technologies, and construction practices to guide the technical design team. The authors researched building and design elements and came up with categories such as materials, ventilation systems, water conservation, recycling, and construction wastes. They made recommendations on everything from proper ground-breaking practices to termite control and photovoltaic applications. They also recommended ways to reduce the indoor air pollutants that can potentially affect the homeowner's health. The *Guide* became a valuable resource for APS and, later, for the architects also,

Some Environmental Terms Defined

1. Green buildings are structures that are designed, constructed, operated, renovated, and demolished in an environmentally and energy-efficient manner. Green building concepts include energy efficiency and conservation, air quality, especially indoor air quality, resources and materials efficiency, environmental performance, and improved environmental quality in the air, water, and on the land.

2. Life cycle assessment (LCA) is a technical, data-based, holistic approach to define and subsequently reduce the environmental burdens associated with a product, process, or activity. By identifying and quantifying energy and material usage and waste discharges, and then assessing the impact of those wastes on the environment, LCA incorporates a "cradle-to-grave" analysis of each product, process, or activity used in construction.

3. A product's "cradle-to-grave" profile begins with a review of its origin, what raw materials are required to make it, where these come from, and how much energy is consumed to make this acquisition. The profile continues through the life of the product until it is either disposed of in the ground, in fire, in water, or is recycled.

4. The embodied energy of a product is the sum of its materials, all of which contain energy used for natural resource extraction, manufacture, transport, installation and, after useful life is over, removal and disposal. A building's embodied-energy investment includes extraction energy, manufacturing energy, transport energy, durability, salvage and reuse, and disposal.

5. Resource efficiency is achieved when fewer natural resources are required to reach a particular goal. Resource-efficient products or materials have low embodied energy, usually because they have been manufactured or produced using the embodied energy of other products that are being recycled.

6. Energy efficiency refers to minimizing the use of energy for space cooling/heating, lighting, and water heating/cooling. It is measured in energy ratings that provide information on the degree to which a feature, product, or device requires energy to perform its function.

7. Transferability is the ability of concepts, products, strategies, and designs that have been developed for one element or situation to be easily applied to other elements or situations.

(From Curran 1994, Bierman-Lytle 1994, O'Brien and Palermini 1993) with many of its recommendations used in the final design of the home.

As the *Design Issues Guide* was being compiled, APS assembled teams of local experts and company personnel to research the various technical aspects of environmentally responsible building. The Work Groups, as they were called, started meeting in December 1992 and presented the results of their research in January 1993. Separate work groups looked at air quality; site work, land use, and water conservation; lighting; and energy and environmental controls. APS officials also took time to visit many environmental homes across the country to acquaint themselves further with their new venture, building an environmental home. Appendix A lists selected environmental homes in the Unites States and Canada by project name, location, and key features.

An important lesson to be learned in understanding environmental homes is that of resource efficiency. Based on the environmental precept of the "3Rs," or "reduce, reuse, and recycle," it means that we should be aware of the entire life-cycle costs of products and materials, such as the embodied energy within a material, or the costs of extracting,

manufacturing, packaging, and even recycling it. Resource efficiency can also refer to how much energy or water is saved when using a product—for instance, a well-insulated wall will not waste the resource that it took to heat or cool the air inside the home. Resource efficiency is the key to understanding environmental building—the resources that we save today will be available for our children to use tomorrow. The project team at APS based their ideals for the home on this important environmental concept.

Choosing the Site

Choosing a site for the home proved to be a lengthy process influenced by several different factors. Among the most important was to search for an urban infill lot. In a city like Phoenix, urban sprawl has covered the desert floor with development upon development, linked by strip shopping centers lining ever-widening streets. The project team felt that it was important not to add to the city's traffic and infrastructure problems by building at the edge of the city. Instead, it looked for an existing

neighborhood with an undeveloped lot that would lend itself to the proposed design. The lot had to allow for an east-west orientation of the long axis of the home for optimum control of sunlight; it also had to have enough land available for creative site development that could showcase alternative building strategies, provide adequate space for parking and the demonstration of xeriscaping and microclimatic landscaping techniques, and offer a buffer for neighbors.

The first location considered for the home was a beautiful hillside lot on the north edge of the Phoenix Mountain Preserve, a pristine area set aside for open space by the city of Phoenix. The project team decided that the lot was too unique: it might dictate the architecture of the home; and its cost was too high: it would not match the development sites favored by the target market of production builders. The second proposed location, in an older neighborhood near the intersection of Central and Maryland avenues, was dismissed because the existing urban fabric could constrain the design of the home. Neighbors there also voiced concerns that APS was making commercial use of a residential lot. The third lot at Tatum

Ranch on the north side of Phoenix was rejected because the developer of the community, SunCor Development Company, is a sister company of APS, and the team felt that this fact could detract from the project potential if misconstrued. The site was also problematic because it lay at the edge of the city limits, and APS officials preferred an infill location that would not add to Phoenix's existing urban sprawl.

The site selection process also included issues unique to this project because of the home's showcase aspects. For example, because a major goal of the project was to demonstrate ways of reducing construction site debris, the site had to be located where builders, construction workers, and new home buyers could see it while driving by, such as in an area of new subdivision growth and building activity. Finally, APS considered drainage factors such as natural washes and other site factors that would create opportunities for passive environmental design strategies.

The fourth site considered, at 60th Street and Greenway Road, met all these criteria. In addition, the existing neighborhood residents supported the development of the home, providing

APS with positive community relations in the area. After this extensive search, APS purchased the lot in June 1993.

An Architect Is Selected

In July 1992, APS began selecting an architect for the ESH. In the first phase of a two-phase process, the company sent out a request for qualifications to all registered Arizona architects. Thirty-six architectural firms indicated interest in the project. A selection panel chose four finalists (Jones Studio, Inc.; William P. Bruder, Architect, Ltd.; Jeffrey Cook, AIA; and Line and Space), who were paid $6,000 each to create full presentations of their design ideas for the home. In November 1992, the jury made the final selection and offered the contract to Jones Studio, Inc. of Phoenix.

Jones Studio was established in 1979 by Edward Jones; his brother Neal joined the firm in 1986 as president and CEO in charge of business and marketing. A third member of the firm, Tom Hahn, has been extensively involved in all phases of the ESH, leading the search for environmentally sensitive building materials and systems.

Phase 2 of selection process: jury considers presentations of finalists

Previous projects by Jones Studio have established the firm as a leader in environmental design and construction techniques. In 1982 the architects experimented with a subterranean energy-efficient home (the Christopher House in Phoenix). In 1985 the Lattimore House in Prescott, Arizona, used solar orientation and an integrated landscape with native vegetation to achieve savings in energy and water.

A recent project, the Black Canyon Trailhead, won several awards including the 1992 Central Arizona Chapter of the American Institute of Architects Honor Award for its use of simple materials, its design clarity, and its use of photovoltaics and composting toilets in an area where power and water are not available from a utility. Another project, the headquarters building of the Arizona Cardinals football team, makes creative use of metal trellises and masonry flue tile screens to create baffles for the direct sunlight that would otherwise strike its west-facing windows. Sophisticated daylighting techniques complement the sun control and bring indirect light deep into the building. This design has won twelve architectural awards since its completion.

When Jones Studio received the commission for the ESH, the staff at the firm launched into research that, according to Edward Jones, continued throughout the design process and construction of the home. To complete the commission, information was needed about the field of recycled and resource-efficient materials; this field proved to be much more extensive than the staff had expected. Because the science and availability of recycled building materials is so new and the applications of the materials change constantly, decisions about selecting materials were difficult to make, sometimes causing delays in the construction as new products were recognized and evaluated. The staff's extensive research will benefit the homebuilding industry by making available the latest information on environmentally sensitive building materials.

Jones Studio: The Spirit of Architecture

To Edward Jones, the principal architect for the home, the underlying question in designing the ESH was how Jones Studio could respond to the ideals of environmentalism while remaining true to what he calls the spirit of architecture. The three Rs—reduce, reuse, and recycle—can place constraints or at least challenges on architectural design objectives. The architect wanted to go beyond a one-dimensional approach to environmental building based largely on resource efficiency and think about the next level of design, which includes quality, lifestyle, space, and architectural meaning.

Jones was influenced early in his career by the works of Frank Lloyd Wright, who had come to Arizona in the 1930s to establish Taliesin West, bringing with him his ideals of organic architecture. His Usonian houses in particular are precursors of the ideals of the ESH. These houses were intended for modern families: they were built with an open plan and minimal ornamentation using low-cost materials, including plywood and concrete block. Wright even designed the furniture for his Usonian houses, using angular lines to save on materials. Jones was also influenced by the Case Study Houses of the 1950s, which were built in California to demonstrate affordable solutions to the postwar housing shortage. These houses,

ranging from 1,700 to 3,500 square feet, emphasized simple, inexpensive materials and the integration of indoor and outdoor spaces, concepts which are to be found in the ESH.

Jones Studio presented its first design for the ESH in November 1992. At that time, the site under consideration was the lot at Central and Maryland, within an older, established neighborhood. Bold and unconventional, the

design solved several problems with an innovative approach.

The design presented consisted of a 3,200-square-foot home, with its long axis oriented east-west on the lot, a sunken garden around and beneath the home, and a roof that opened up to the sky like a set of butterfly wings. Though the garden did not find its way into the final design, a variation of the butterfly roof can be seen on the present garage.

Jones considered the butterfly roof an elegant solution to several problems faced by environmental homes. First, the V-shaped roof did an excellent job accommodating the photovoltaic panels, the devices that collect solar rays and turn them into electricity. It provided 1,000 square feet of surface area at an optimum angle for the photovoltaic panels to collect those rays at all times of the year, while at the same time

Original design for the ESH, by Jones Studio, Inc.

15

hiding the panels from view. Second, it functioned as a rainwater collector, channeling rain into a single gutter and directing it to storage for landscape irrigation. Third, the roof form was the ceiling form, which allowed the south daylight to diffuse evenly and deeply throughout the house. Fourth, the curve of the ceiling/roof could exhaust warmer air by natural convection, allowing it to rise to the high point of the roof and be vented outside.

The sunken garden was to be constructed like a basement, except that it would be a protected outdoor living space enhanced by an environmentally responsible pool design. The pool water could be aerated by letting it overflow and recirculate to the sunken garden. A built-in fan would force air through the waterfall, producing an evaporative cooling effect. Floor intake grilles allowed the cooler garden air to be pulled into the natural convection currents of the house.

The swimming pool was therefore a place for recreation, a visual focal point, and an air conditioner, another example of making one design feature serve several functions. This concept of a feature having more than one function is an inportant design element that can also be found in the current ESH.

The butterfly roof and the sunken garden of the first design were creative design solutions to the problems of building in the desert. However, APS's ultimate goal was to appeal to the average homebuilder and home buyer. The target audience might construe Jones Studio's first design as too radical and futuristic and dismiss it out of hand. In fact, residential neighbors near the proposed site did oppose the roof design.

Because a showcase home needs to be acceptable to a large number of people, the project team worked toward a more conventional design. Jones felt that changing the design of the home did not necessarily have to adversely affect the integrity of the final outcome. In a conversation with the authors of this book, Jones stated that,

> The design kept evolving. What I'm really proud of is that the house has been able to respond to a different set of criteria that developed subsequent to the competition. There was a different site chosen, different materials evaluated, a lot of changes, but the final design accepted those changes without compromising the design integrity. If the fundamental concept is strong and sincerely prototypical, then it can respond to variations.

Jones also pointed out that his firm was "interested in trying to address the issue of environmentalism both directly and indirectly." He hoped to go beyond the usual materials-driven and energy-efficient construction methods of environmental homes and provide another approach to environmental building. Jones explained that, in addition to developing a quantitative description of an environmental home, focusing on solar gain, traffic patterns, R-values, embodied energy, mechanical systems, and other factors that can be counted and charted, he wanted to create a home that would provide quality of life.

Jones concentrated on the sculptural elements of the home: the indoor and outdoor spaces, the relationship of living areas to one another, the flow of daylight into every room, and the scale of the home. "I wanted every element to contribute something to that sculpture as well as to technical requirements. Every component had to address those two issues; otherwise, the decision was revisited."

Design Features of the Home: Sun Sponges and a Glass Wall

A cross section of the final home design shows how the home incorporates environmentally sensitive design features into a sensible, livable structure that welcomes the family into its living spaces. Unlike many experimental resource-efficient homes, the environmental aspects of this home enhance rather than sacrifice the comfort of the inhabitants. A review of the design features shows how this is done.

As with all good home designs, the home did not start with the floor plan but with the site plan. An architect must take into consideration the topography, the surrounding areas and sightlines, and any existing constraints before he or she can determine how the home will relate to those factors. Foremost in this process was the orientation of the home: it needed to be sited with its long axis in an east-west direction, with the living areas facing south, to allow for maximum sun/shade control. Desert societies throughout history have accommodated the angle of the sun's rays in their structures. Only in latter-day industrial times have we been able to override this constraint and compensate for the higher heat factor in our homes by producing cool air mechanically. This switch in emphasis from good design to artificial cooling has resulted not only in higher energy costs, but also in higher environmental costs because of the pollution released while generating power and the environmental impact of building electricity-generating power plants. With its east-west orientation and other design factors, the ESH demonstrates how a home's design is as important as its materials in conserving energy.

Another important consideration was returning the indigenous desert to areas of the lot not taken up by the footprint of the home. Originally, the designers hoped to save any indigenous plants and return them to the site after construction was complete. However, when the present site was selected, it was obvious that the indigenous vegetation had long ago been stripped from the site, and years of dumping of soil from other areas had degraded the topsoil and raised the height of the lot. Several feet of soil had to be removed in order that the completed home would be on the same level as the surrounding homes and not block their views.

Cross section of the final design for the ESH, by Jones Studio, Inc.

Main entrance

However, in spite of these constraints, the landscaping of the home was designed to restore the original desert environment as much as possible.

The home itself is approached from the north side. There is a subtle transition from the outdoor area to the indoor, a theme that is repeated throughout the home. As you approach the front door, you go from entirely outside to partially outside, through a gate, and finally to the front door. This handling of the entrance contrasts with the typical subdivision home, whose front door symbolizes a distinct line of demarcation—you are either inside or outside. In the ESH, you enter through a series of inviting, welcoming spaces that lead to a sheltering environment. This attention to the personal experience of the home's occupants and visitors is at the heart of the home's design strategy.

Other areas of the home blur the division between the inside and outside. The pool area, located on the south side of the home, can be opened up completely to the living area through an ingenious sliding patio door so large it becomes a glass wall. Unlike a typical arcadia door, half of which slides and stacks over the other half when opened, this glass wall disappears, sliding along the outside wall of the home. The result is a completely open space available for indoor/outdoor use. With the glass wall closed, the view of the outside, with its small grassy area, pool, and desert landscaping, becomes a part of the interior, as important to the living room design as the furniture.

The integration of the indoor and outdoor spaces can be understood in purely visual terms. As one moves through the home, translucency alternates with transparency and opacity to create a shifting range of elements, allowing both privacy and shared experiences to occur within the same set of walls. The result is that feelings of mystery and anticipation are part of one's understanding of the home.

A noticeable external feature of the home is the fabric baffles protecting the high clerestory windows. Tom Hahn refers to them as "sun sponges," because they are designed to block the sun's heat while absorbing and transmitting its light into the living areas of the home. Three feet wide and six feet high, they hang perpendicular to the glass eight feet apart, acting as vertical shades and deflecting the sun's rays from the glass during the hottest part of the summer. They are only one of a series of steel-and-fabric structures surrounding the home that absorb heat while transmitting light.

There are four main outdoor living spaces, each oriented to one of the four compass points. Fabric and louvered sunshades at all four outdoor areas are used to control heat gain, extending the roofline another fifteen feet on each side. Each of these outdoor living areas is designed to have different qualities at different times of the year, enabling future residents to experience a maximum amount of time outdoors if they so choose. As in ancient and modern desert structures in other parts of the world, the walls of the home accomplish a dual purpose: not only do they protect the interior of the home, they also provide shelter for activities occurring on the exterior.

The south side of the home represents the main living area. On this side, the fabric shade is totally retractable. In the summer, the residents can have the shade fully extended, providing a covered patio suitable for poolside activities. In the winter, with the shade retracted, the sun warms the patio and

the adjacent living room. The residents can roll out the shade in varying degrees, depending on the sun's position and their needs. The fabric itself softens and transmits the sunlight to the area below. This built-in flexibility enhances the livability of the home.

An important feature of the ESH is its use of daylighting, the technique whereby the natural light of day is allowed to enter and illuminate the interior spaces. Other environmental homes that have been built over the past few years have attempted to control the sun's rays by installing small windows or by berming, with the result that many of them have a sunless, underground feeling to them. The public may think of environmental homes as unpleasantly dark inside and not suitable for current lifestyles, which are centered around enjoying the outdoors. Jones Studio wanted to turn that impression around by designing a home that was environmentally sensitive and energy efficient, but still filled with light.

The architects accomplished that goal with the north-facing clerestory windows along the entire length of the home, which are protected in the summer by the sun sponges. In a typical home, the roof pitches downward from

From above: **Sun sponges, mechanical plenum during construction, fabric shade being installed over patio**

Right: Detail of garage roof rainwater collector
Below: Change in roof pitch, showing the clerestory space
Opposite page: Living area with clerestory windows

a center line. In the ESH, the roof pitch changes partway up the south side—it kicks up and climbs another 5 feet toward the sky. On the north side of this changed roofline is the clerestory—a series of motorized, operable windows that provide soft northern daylight and natural ventilation to the interior of the home. An ingenious reflector system, described below, bounces the light into the living areas.

The reflector is actually a mechanical plenum spline made of gypsum board. Splines sometimes exist in homes to accommodate the mechanical ductwork and electrical wiring, but in this home the spline also functions as a daylight reflector. Supported throughout the length of the home by metal framing, the triangular structure seems to float below the clerestory windows, evenly distributing the daylight from above. The northern light bounces off its white surface and is reflected into every living area of the home, allowing the inhabitants always to have natural light during the daytime hours. This simple yet sophisticated design feature also saves energy, first by reducing the need for artificial light, and second by making the best use of available daylight

without sacrificing reduced window exposure. It is an excellent example of how the design of the ESH is as important as the materials it is made from when it comes to conserving energy.

Inside the home, the daylight spills from room to room through interior "windows" that carry light and space from one interior area to another. For several of the inside walls, the architects have installed glass transoms high on the walls, allowing an indirect visual connection between rooms. The result is a visual expansion of the space inside the home—usually boxy rooms become open and spacious because the occupant can see beyond their confines.

The clerestory windows have another purpose besides letting daylight into the home; they can be opened to allow air movement. When opened, they can draw air from the area outside the living room, where during the spring and fall, when the nights cool quickly, a patch of grass and the fabric overhang produce cooler air than that inside the home . Convection currents gently draw fresh, cool air through the opened glass wall of the living room and circulate it through the home. As this occurs, the warm inside air rises and vents out at the highest point of the home—the opened windows of the clerestory. The natural ventilation created by this design forestalls the use of energy-intensive air conditioning for several weeks in the spring and fall.

In addition to allowing daylight into the home, the roof design fulfills an important energy-saving function. On the south side of the home, the roof is placed at an optimum angle to gather the sun's rays for the solar water heaters and the photovoltaic collectors. Photovoltaic collectors absorb solar radiation and convert it into electricity for the home's occupants. Their function is explained more fully in chapter 2.

The roof also functions as an active rainwater collector. The home has four points of collection: as the rain hits the roof surface, it is collected in gutters that carry it into four catch basins at the corners of the home. The catch basins are circular concrete slabs with grates that allow the water to enter subsurface pipes that lead to an underground storage system. The rainwater is stored, then added to the gray water collected from inside the home and used for landscape irrigation by means of an automated, underground drip system.

The butterfly roof concept originally proposed for the home eventually found its way (somewhat modified) to the garage, contributing to another system of rainwater harvesting. The water collects in a gutter that runs down the center of the garage roof and leads to an aboveground cistern located next to the vegetable garden. A hose is attached to the bottom of the cistern, and the owner simply turns the spigot to use the saved water to grow vegetables. This is the simplest and most affordable means of water harvesting: no underground pipes and storage tanks are required, the expense is minimal, and potable water is conserved. An extra design feature has been added to the garage roof by replacing the bottom of the gutter with a piece of glass. The glass acts as a linear skylight for the garage (which will be a visitors' center while the home is on display) and allows the viewer to see firsthand the concept behind rainwater harvesting. This and other water-saving features are explained in chapter 3.

The materials from which the home is constructed are as environmentally sensitive as its design. Much of the floor, for example, is made of a special concrete that contains flyash, a byproduct of

Environmental Showcase Home (ESH)

APS's coal-fired electricity production that is usually treated as waste. Adding the flyash to the concrete diverts it from the landfill and uses it to strengthen the foundation of the home. Months of research by the ESH team into the latest construction materials available for environmentally responsible building led to this and other innovative features. Descriptions of the various building materials and how they were selected are in chapter 4.

The final chapter of the book considers the ESH as part of the current movement of sustainable design and summarizes its effect on energy use and air pollution. An epilogue describes how

a subdivision of homes based on the ESH design might look.

As described in this chapter, the home's design makes use of some features that could be seen as unusual in the current homebuilding market. Some may question the transferability to production homebuilding of features such as the clerestory windows, with their complex array of reflectors and interior windows, or the east-west orientation of the home. But some of these design features, which at first may appear exaggerated, function well as graphic communicators of environmental homebuilding ideas. Edward Jones has said, "we have not departed radically from

standard forms. It's still simple span beams, columns, windows, doors, walls, roof, and an economical repetitive structure, the same components production homebuilders have always worked with."

The most comprehensive environmental feature of the ESH is its design. A home's design must respond to human needs for light, comfort, space, and a sense of belonging. The ESH, while fulfilling APS's goals and objectives in producing an environmentally sensitive home, also contains what Edward Jones called the spirit of architecture, creating a home that is not only environmentally responsible, but architecturally sensible.

Sources

Arizona Public Service Company. n.d. The Arizona Environmental Strategic Alliance. Pamphlet. Phoenix, AZ.

———. 1992. Environmental Showcase Home: Marketing Plan. Final Draft.

Bierman-Lytle, Paul. "Environmental Building Materials: What are they? Where are they?" *U.S. Green Building Conference—1994.* Washington, DC: Government Printing Office.

Curran, Mary Ann. 1994. "Life Cycle Assessment." *U.S. Green Building Conference—1994.* Washington, DC: Government Printing Office.

DeMichele, Mark. 1994. Interview with David Pijawka.

EcoGroup, Inc., and Center for Resourceful Building Technology. 1993. *Design Issues Guide.* Tempe, AZ.

Gifford, J. Brent. 1994. Interview with David Pijawka.

Hahn, Tom. 1994. "The Environmental Showcase Home." *Recycling Review.*

Jones, Edward. 1994. Interview with David Pijawka.

Jones, Neal. 1994. Firm Profile of Jones Studio, Inc. Phoenix, AZ.

Jones Studio, Inc. 1994. *Environmental Showcase Home Project Narrative.* Phoenix, AZ

Loken, Steve, Walter Spurling, and Carol Price. 1993. *Guide to Resource Efficient Building Elements.* Missoula, MT: Center for Resourceful Building Technology.

O'Brien, Michael and Debbi Palermini. 1993. *Guide to Resource Efficient Building.* Portland, OR: The Sustainable Building Collaborative.

Westgroup Marketing Research. 1992. *Environmental Home Focus Groups.* Phoenix, AZ.

2
Energy Efficiency

Builders of single-family homes in the southwestern United States must contend with extremes of climate unlike those in any other part of the country. In Phoenix, temperatures can range from freezing temperature to 122 degrees Fahrenheit. The intense sunlight presents a challenge to homebuilders in preventing solar heat gain in the summer but it also provides an opportunity to use solar-based technologies. Since the advent of air conditioning in the 1950s, home design in the Southwest has hardly acknowledged the climate extremes of the desert environment.

If homes in the Valley were designed to take advantage of the sun's energy and to avoid the summer's extreme heat, we would be able to save a tremendous amount of energy presently coming from nonrenewable sources. With its passive solar design, insulated home envelope, active low-energy systems, and active solar technologies, the Environmental Showcase Home is an example of efficient energy use through proper design. Energy-saving features and systems, listed in table 2, show the range of techniques currently available to today's homebuilders. Using only the first three categories listed, annual electricity use would be reduced by 60 percent over a typical home. The home's designers then added active solar technology (solar water heating and photovoltaics), resulting in a savings of 80 percent. This chapter will show how the home's energy-saving features work to bring about these results.

Opposite page:
Photovoltaic cells

Passive solar design	
Orientation	East-west axis with the living areas facing south
Shading	Use of overhangs, "sun sponges," patio trellises, landscaping
Venting	High venting at clerestory for passive ventilation; operable glass; stacking window patio system to open interior to exterior
Landscaping	Landscape designed to protect home from direct and reflected solar radiation in summer but to allow penetration in winter
Paving materials	Special materials selected for paving to minimize "heat sink" effect of driveways
Daylighting	Design of home allows natural light to enter without corresponding heat gain

Home envelope	
Fenestration (window system)	Lower window-to-floor space ratio; thermally broken frames; use of low-emissivity film, high-rating glazing systems; very high R-values; argon gas in multi-paned systems
Thermal mass	Medium thermal mass in interior living areas of the home
Insulation	Use of high levels of insulation
Exterior walls	High insulation due to polyurethane in concrete masonry
Air leakage control	Weather stripping, sill sealers, caulking, housewrap, extensive use of sealants

Active low-energy systems	
Heating, ventilating, and air conditioning	Two triple-function heat pumps
Heat pump water heater	Saves 17 percent of typical water heater energy costs
Fluorescent lighting	More energy-efficient than conventional lighting systems
Control zones	Home divided into separately controlled temperature zones

Active solar systems	
Photovoltaic application	Photovoltaic panels to help share peak electricity requirements for the ESH
Solar water heater	Simple system can generate nearly all of the hot water needs

2. Energy-saving design features and systems of the ESH

The Importance of Energy Conservation

Though some sources of energy—like the sun or the wind—are classified as renewable energy sources, the great bulk of our usable energy is provided by nonrenewable or finite resources such as coal, oil, and natural gas, which will eventually be used up. When the world was less populated, the available usable energy seemed almost limitless. With the advent of industrial development and an increasing world population, these same resources are not stretching nearly as far as before.

The utility industry, which relies on many of these resources, contributes to the problem. With annual revenues of about $800 billion, it is one of the world's largest industries—about twice the size of the automobile industry—and the world's largest consumer of fossil fuels. Power plants, particularly the coal-fired plants that provide nearly 40 percent of the world's electricity, are also large polluters. They contribute nearly one-third of the atmospheric concentrations of carbon dioxide, as much as to two-thirds of sulfur dioxide (a major air pollutant), and emissions of

heavy metals. Fossil fuel combustion is emitting heat-trapping carbon dioxide at a rate of what could equal 5.9 billion tons of carbon per year.

Although experts disagree, some claim that the resulting buildup of carbon dioxide threatens to warm the atmosphere (referred to as the "greenhouse effect"), alter agricultural and weather patterns, and disrupt natural ecosystems. Reducing the generation of electrical energy would lessen this impact on the environment.

Figure 3 shows the major sources of electrical power at the national and state (Arizona) level by percentage. The use of coal, long the world's largest easily available energy source, appears to be slowing, although coal still provides half of Arizona's electrical energy. An abundant and relatively inexpensive energy source, it is also the dirtiest of the fuel sources and contributes heavily to environmental damage. Arizona, like the nation, is primarily dependent on coal for electricity production. The typical coal-fired plant in the United States emits into the atmosphere 1.29 grams of nitrogen oxide, 17.2 grams of sulfur, and 884 grams of carbon dioxide per kWh of energy produced. Today's largest source

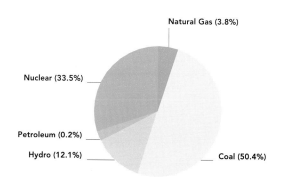

Natural Gas (3.8%)
Nuclear (33.5%)
Petroleum (0.2%)
Hydro (12.1%)
Coal (50.4%)

Arizona, 1990

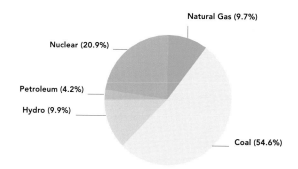

Natural Gas (9.7%)
Nuclear (20.9%)
Petroleum (4.2%)
Hydro (9.9%)
Coal (54.6%)

United States, 1990

3. Energy input mix for electric power generation

Source: U.S. Department of Energy, (1992)

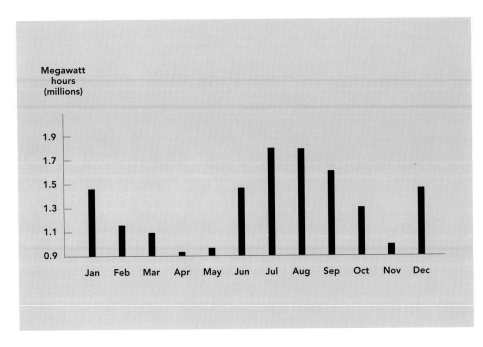

Megawatt hours (millions)

1.9
1.7
1.5
1.3
1.1
0.9

Jan Feb Mar Apr May Jun Jul Aug Sep Oct Nov Dec

4. Arizona residential electricity use

of renewable energy, hydroelectric power, provides more than 20 percent of the world's electricity and about 12 percent of Arizona's electricity. Hydropower emits no carbon dioxide and little pollution, but the dams that are built to generate hydropower can destroy wildlife habitats, cause soil erosion, and lead to a loss of productivity of downstream rivers. Geothermal, wind, and solar energy could one day provide a substantial amount of the world's electricity and produce limited, if any, air or water pollution.

It is estimated that the amount of solar energy reaching the earth's surface each year totals more than 10,000 times the electricity used by all human beings each year. Some of this energy can be converted into electricity with the relatively new technology of photovoltaic cells. Though not used commercially until the 1970s, photovoltaic cells now produce enough electricity worldwide to meet a diverse array of power needs. The generation of electricity from photovoltaics creates no air pollution and yields little waste. One drawback of the technology is that the production of the solar cells themselves may cause some pollution.

About 20 percent of all energy consumption in the United States is for residential use and, of this, 80 percent is used for space heating and cooling. It is astounding that Arizona, having one of the highest rates of insolation in the country, falls behind other states in the per capita use of solar installations. Arizona's population has grown so rapidly that even though the per capita energy use has declined, the total amount of energy consumed in the state has increased by 41.6 percent between 1973 and 1992. Much can be done to improve the efficient use of energy in the state, including cutting down on residential energy use and taking advantage of the solar energy available throughout the year.

One of the factors that influences energy demand is peak energy use (figure 4). This is especially true in Arizona because in the low desert, peak levels of energy demand occur in the summer months of July, August, and September, when air conditioners and swimming pool equipment require high amounts of electricity. Utility companies must expend a significant amount of capital in facility expansion just to meet these peak levels. Much of this peak demand can be mitigated through passive energy design strategies. For example, the ESH uses such strategies as energy-efficient insulation, shading, appropriate windows, natural lighting, ventilation, and site orientation.

Peak levels of energy demand also occur during the hottest parts of the day. Transferring electricity use from peak to nonpeak hours in the summer not only benefits the environment, but often saves money on monthly utility bills because many companies charge less for electricity during nonpeak periods. The ESH was designed to demonstrate the effects of energy-efficient technologies and systems that will reduce the effects of energy use during peak demand periods.

Energy-Saving Components of the ESH

Low-Energy-Use Systems and Appliances

The high-performance energy-efficient systems of the ESH cause it to use nearly 60 percent less energy than that of a typical new home. The ESH adopts top-of-the-line environmental

products to educate the public and to demonstrate innovative energy systems. As a showcase home, its purpose is not to test new ideas in energy reduction or to incorporate unusual design elements unavailable to the general public. Rather, the home demonstrates systems and materials currently available on the market. The following components from the ESH demonstrate how energy can be saved throughout an environmentally conscious home.

Two heating, ventilating, and air conditioning (HVAC) systems are featured in the ESH, though either one could be used alone in a typical home. The primary operating system, the Intertherm PowerMiser by Nordyne, is a triple-function heat pump that not only heats and cools the home, but also heats water efficiently. With the PowerMiser, the amount of energy required to generate hot water for a three-person household is estimated to be 360 kWh per year, a savings of about 80 percent over a typical water heater. When compared to minimum federal standards for air conditioners alone (SEER 10), the system is about 20 percent more efficient. (SEER, or Seasonal Energy Efficiency Rating, is a way of measuring the energy

efficiency of a product: the higher the number, the less energy it uses.) According to the manufacturer, when water heating is added to its air cooling and heating functions, the system's total energy efficiency may be even higher, perhaps equivalent to a SEER 20.

The second HVAC unit, located in the demonstration area in the garage, is the Trane Super Efficiency heat pump system, with a SEER rating of 14. While units with higher SEER ratings are available, this particular unit was selected because it offers features suitable to a desert environment. For example, SEER ratings are based on an air temperature of 82 degrees Fahrenheit. In Arizona, however, summer temperatures routinely exceed 82 degrees Fahrenheit, often by 20 to 25 degrees. During these periods, air conditioner efficiency usually falls, and units with ratings above SEER 14 are not as efficient at higher peak temperatures.

For example, the Energy Efficiency Rating (EER), the measure of a unit's efficiency at a specific point in time, for a SEER 14 unit is 12.6 at 115 degrees, while a SEER 16.5 unit has an EER of only 9.9 at the same temperature. Therefore, the SEER 14 system is more

A super efficiency heat pump

Type of appliance	Brand name	Advantage	Energy saved (kWh)	Savings over standard equipment (%)
Refrigerator	Whirlpool SERP	Energy efficient; also has a CFC-free sealed compressor system and CFC-free insulation	300	30
Clothes washer	Westinghouse LT 350R	Energy efficient because of horizontal axis design (front-loading); less energy required to heat a smaller amount of water	80	33
Dishwasher	Amana DU7500	Designed to use as few as 8 gallons of water per load	250	70
Induction rangetop	GE Profile JP393R	Cooktop remains cool during cooking	40	10
Convection/thermal microwave	Thermador CMT-227 Combination Unit	Combination unit saves resource material; also vents air directly outside	100	30
		Total Savings (kWh)	770	

5. Energy savings from selected ESH appliances

effective than the SEER 16.5 system on peak days during the summer season.

The ESH demonstrates three different water-heating systems, though any one could be used alone in a typical home to save energy. In addition to the heat pump system described above, which generates hot water efficiently, there is also a solar water-heating system. The Copper Cricket can provide nearly 100 percent of the ESH's water-heating needs. It is a thermal "geyser-pumping action" device that uses a solar collector to heat a water/alcohol-based solution. The heated fluid flows

to a heat exchanger in a water storage tank where it gives up its heat to the potable water. While there is an efficiency loss in the heat exchange, the geyser action principle eliminates the need for pumps powered by electricity. The solution used in the panel and heat exchanger is freeze-proof and nontoxic. The collector is recognized as highly efficient, with the ability to gather heat on even marginally sunny days.

The availability of sunshine in Phoenix permits this system to operate year round except for the few consecutive cloudy days each year. This system

can save over 2,000 kWh in water heating, an amount required to heat water for a family of three annually.

A third water heater was chosen for display only in the garage area. Using heat pump technology, it heats water efficiently and also provides cool air that could be directed into a home's ductwork to help offset cooling energy use.

To reduce the energy needed to heat water, it is also possible to reduce the amount of hot water used. The installation of low-water-use appliances or low-flow fixtures for activities that require hot water, such as hand and dish washing, provides significant environmental benefits. The impact of these features alone on water use in the ESH is shown in the next chapter on water conservation.

The energy-efficient appliances in the ESH were carefully selected for their energy- and water-savings potential and avoidance of environmentally harmful chemicals such as CFCs. Low-water-use appliances mean that less water has to be heated to do the same job, resulting in less use of energy. Table 5 shows the results of an APS analysis on the amount of energy saved using the chosen products as compared to appliances typically found in households today. When these energy-efficient appliances are used exclusively, an estimated savings of 770 kWh will be realized over energy-inefficient appliances.

A typical home uses around 1,300 kWh for lighting. The ESH lighting systems were designed to reduce that figure by 50 percent with the extensive use of fluorescent technology combined with halogen lights in appropriate areas. To use daylight effectively, the home features north-facing clerestory windows that allow the sun to replace artificial light during most of the day.

One feature that was not used in the ESH would have added to its energy efficiency. Comprehensive home automation systems are currently becoming more economical and could have allowed for more integration of the various systems of the home to improve energy efficiency.

Solar Technologies

Many of us think that the use of solar power to meet energy needs is a relatively new technology. Actually, it is one of the oldest energy sources to be used. The Romans set up atriums or courtyards to take advantage of the warmth of the sun. The prehistoric Anasazi built their pueblos in south-facing caves and rock overhangs, providing shade in the summer heat and warmth from the sun in the winter cold. These are examples of passive solar design, used in designing homes for thousands of years.

The ESH uses several passive solar techniques to save energy. The most important is the east-west orientation of the home, with its living areas facing south. This orientation allows for the most efficient use of the sun's heat in the winter, while shielding the living areas in the summer. Another way to

Energy-saving appliances in the ESH kitchen

Solar water heater

take advantage of solar energy is by using the sun's rays to produce heat or other types of energy. By combining what we know of the sun's movement with our ability to design and produce highly sophisticated components, we can expand the ways we use the sun's energy through active solar technology. The ESH demonstrates two major types of active solar energy technologies: solar water heaters and photovoltaic cells. Both make good use of Arizona's solar bounty.

Solar water-heating technology is well established and used extensively today in Florida and California. It has been used in Phoenix since 1917, when it was installed on the historic Shackleford House. During the period from 1891 to 1930, it was one of the most popular forms of energy for states blessed with sunshine; only after electricity became less expensive and more readily available in the 1940s did the use of solar water heating decline.

Solar water-heating technology is relatively simple: an active system with solar roof panels absorbs the sun's heat and transfers the heat to the water. This technique is frequently used to preheat water, followed by a boost added by another heater that provides backup and heating for cloudy days. Solar water heaters require little maintenance—an annual checkup is all they normally need—and can supply up to 70 percent of a home's electric demand for heating water. However, the system described above, the Copper Cricket solar water heater, can generate almost 100 percent of the home's hot water needs. The pool also makes use of solar power for heating water. The Heliocol system, described in chapter 3, heats the pool water efficiently and extends the time the pool can be used.

Photovoltaic energy was discovered in 1839 by French scientist Edmond Becquerel, who discovered that light falling on certain materials can produce electricity. Today, photovoltaic solar cells convert the sun's energy into usable electric power. Although the high price of photovoltaic cells has discouraged their use in the average home, the technology is being successfully used in other areas. For the past twenty-five years, photovoltaic energy has been used to provide electrical power to satellites and other spacecraft. However, until the oil crisis of 1973, there was little interest in using this alternative fuel for less exotic purposes. By 1975, government funding for research and development programs aimed at making photovoltaic use economical had become available. Today, photovoltaic energy powers water pumps, radio repeaters, remote weather-monitoring stations, and home electrical needs in areas where regular electrical service is difficult and expensive to install (including some areas in rural Arizona).

Photovoltaic solar cells convert sunlight directly into electricity (direct current). After an invertor converts direct current (DC) to alternating current (AC), the electricity is ready for use by regular home appliances. The system also has batteries that are able to store electricity for use during the night or during cloudy conditions.

The solar cells are made of silicon, the world's second most abundant element, making up 28 percent of the earth's crust. In its raw state, silicon is simply sand. The major cost of using photovoltaic technology comes from processing the raw sand into a silicon material that is 99.99 percent pure. Much of the research today is directed at finding ways to produce and use an amorphous silicon (or thin-film silicon)

that costs less to manufacture but still produces a relatively high cell efficiency. Improvements in cell efficiency are being made at a rapid rate. In 1990, the thin-film silicon modules were only 3.5 to 5 percent efficient. By 1992 the rate was up to 5 to 6 percent; in 1994 it was reported that a new photovoltaic solar cell had been developed with an efficiency of 10.2 percent, a current record for thin-film silicon.

While efficiency is rising, we are also seeing a decrease in the cost of using photovoltaic technology. In 1950, the cost of photovoltaic use was $600 per watt; by 1990 that cost had come down to $8.50 per watt. The latest amorphous silicon solar cells being developed may soon be incorporated into roofing shingles during construction and should be able to supply a home with electricity at an acceptable cost to the homeowner. It is projected that this technology will be cost-effective enough for the average consumer shortly after the year 2000.

The technology for incorporating photovoltaics into roofing shingles was still being developed when the APS team was deciding what photovoltaic system to use in the ESH. Instead of using the new shingles, the team chose

Installation of photovoltaic cells *Background:* **photovoltaic cells on roof of home**

Number of cells or modules	Item powered by photovoltaics	Electricity produced at peak output
1 small cell (1"x 2")	Calculator	0.1 watt
1 standard cell (4"x 4")	Small yard light	0.5 watt
110 modules (47 watts each)	A 1,500–1,800-square-foot home with an evaporative cooler, no air conditioner	5.2 kilowatts
169 modules	Same home with an air conditioner	8 kilowatts
2,600 modules	Solar One, a 24-home subdivision in Glendale, Arizona	192 kilowatts (PV system provides only part of the total power)
58,000 modules	SUMD PV-1 and PV-2 photovoltaic central power plant in California	2 megawatts

6. Number of photovoltaic cells or modules needed to power various applications

a more conventional, roof-mounted system. The ESH uses forty-two photovoltaic modules, each approximately 44 inches by 20 inches, that generate a total of 2.7 kW of electricity.

These modules are connected to the invertor and instrumentation in the utility room, which is then connected to the APS photovoltaic kWh meter on the outside of the home. The cells are tilted 18.4 degrees to provide an optimum angle to the sun. This tilt increases the output in May through August when the need is highest (peak demand), but it lowers the overall annual energy production somewhat. The overall annual production would have been increased by using a tilt of 33.4 degrees, but increasing both summer output and total annual production cannot be satisfied by the same tilt angle. Because the goal was to offset as much summer peak energy as possible, winter energy production was sacrificed. As a general reference, table 6 shows the number of cells or modules needed to provide electrical power for a variety of items.

Already, there are homes in Phoenix, Tucson, Flagstaff, Tempe, and Yuma that are powered by photovoltaic systems. The homes are also connected to the local electric utility system through what is called a "grid connection." The homes use their photovoltaic systems to generate electricity for their needs and sell any excess power back to the utility company (which the utility company must, by law, buy). When the photovoltaic system does not generate enough power to meet consumer demand, electricity can be drawn from the power grid. In addition to the homes using grid-connection photovoltaic technology, there are also 1,200 Arizona homes off-grid (receiving no additional power from utility companies). Most of these homes are on the Navajo and Hopi reservations, where running traditional electric lines could cost from $5,000 to $30,000 per mile.

The technologies of solar water heating and photovoltaic panels help the ESH make use of Arizona's extensive solar power. The solar and other energy-efficient technology applications in the ESH will save around $1,100 per year in energy bills and have a peak demand reduction of 3.2 kW. Although the technology to produce solar power is not currently as inexpensive as other methods of producing energy, the benefits of using solar power are being recognized.

Using solar energy can produce dramatic improvements to our environment and, with it, our quality of life.

The Thermal Envelope

Energy use reduction in home design is centered on the quality and efficiency of a home's exterior walls, which are collectively known as its thermal envelope, or building shell. The integrated thermal envelope includes all of the home's key exterior systems: wall construction (insulation), roof construction, doors, and fenestration (windows).

A key issue in designing homes for passive energy savings is that the thermal mass of the home should be appropriate for the climate. High-mass environmentally conscious homes, as in New Mexico, are built with thick adobe walls that absorb daytime heat and radiate warmth back into the homes during the cool evenings of fall and winter. In Phoenix, where summer nights are often extremely warm, the high thermal mass of thick adobe walls is inappropriate; during the heat of the summer, the massive walls would add heat to the interior of the home, when cooling is desired. High thermal mass may, however, be appropriate in outlying areas at higher

elevations, where the evenings are generally cooler.

For a low-desert environment such as the Phoenix metropolitan area, homes are best built with medium mass to be energy efficient. A medium mass home can be made of masonry, or wood or steel framing, with the mass provided by an extra thick floor slab or insulation in the walls. These heavier walls or floor slabs can store heat or coolness for long periods of time and slowly transfer them back to their surroundings, providing passive solar "tempering" of the indoor air temperature. The energy savings attributable to a well-insulated medium mass home occur by shifting energy consumption to the nighttime and early morning in the summer and the daytime hours in the winter, hours when demand for energy is less and the cost is cheaper.

Much of the ESH is composed of uncovered concrete slabs and tile floors whose medium thermal mass creates energy-saving effects. The large movable glass patio door on the southern exposure enhances this solar tempering strategy. The ability of this glass to reduce heat transfer while transmitting light prevents heat from entering the house during the summer. When the sun

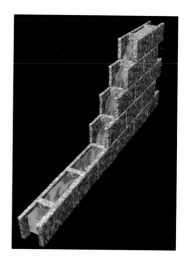

Cutaway of concrete masonry unit showing foam insulation

is at a low angle in the winter months and sunlight can enter directly, it warms the uncovered concrete, which then retains the sun's heat throughout the early evening hours.

The greatest portion of the ESH's thermal envelope is composed of the material of the wall structure. The home uses an 8-inch foam-insulated concrete masonry wall unit known as Integra Block, manufactured by Superlite, a local company. According to the home's architects, "Integra has the highest insulative values of any insulated concrete masonry system we evaluated, primarily because of its special design that eliminates much of the web and its related 'thermal bridging' that also permits more insulation in the cavity."

When injected with foam insulation, Integra Block has an R-value of 24, a substantial increase over R-19, the minimum insulation for a 6-inch wall as recommended by the Energy Office of the Arizona State Department of Commerce. Integra's standard insulation foam was replaced with Supergreen Foam, a polyurethane foam that does not depend on a blowing agent with chlorine-containing chlorofluorocarbons (CFCs) or hydrochlorofluorocarbons

Above: **Concrete masonry units with insulation**
Right: **Concrete masonry units**

(HCFCs), which have been implicated in atmospheric ozone depletion. Supergreen, blown with a compound known as HFC-134a, has no known potential for depleting the earth's ozone. Supergreen is one of the first expanding polyurethane foams in the United States to use HFC-134a—it expands upon installation to effectively seal all pores and voids in the masonry blocks. It also has high insulation values, R-6.5 per inch, protecting the home in the summer and saving cooling energy.

High-value insulation materials have also been placed in the home's roof and in the wood-framed wall sections of the home (Nature Guard), the garage roof and walls (air krete insulation), and the perimeter slab (AMOFOAM RCY insulation). The perimeter slab insulation minimizes heat gain from the soil near the perimeter of the building due to temperature differences between the home and the soil.

Nature Guard insulation, used in the walls and attic of the ESH, is manufactured from cellulose (primarily from recycled newspaper) and is blown dry into attics and wet into wall cavities. Its R-value is 3.8 per inch, higher than most fiberglass products currently available.

The 10 inches of insulation in the roof provides an R-value of 38, an improvement over the minimum 30 recommended by the Energy Office of the Arizona State Department of Commerce. More details on the properties of the ESH's insulative materials can be found in chapter 4.

Insulation "dams" have been inserted between the roof deck and the ceiling insulation, leaving a space of approximately 2 inches. The space provides a path for air to flow from the ventilation holes in the eaves to the ridge vents. The convective air currents set in motion by heat from the roof convey much of the heat away before it reaches the insulation.

The insulation dams are faced with a radiant barrier material composed of an aluminum-coated structural substrate that reflects 95 percent of the heat reaching its surface. Though they have been a subject of much controversy, mainly because of overstated claims, radiant barriers aid in cooling, but the degree of effectiveness and the cost versus benefits are hard to quantify. When a radiant barrier can be installed for a relatively low cost, such as in this case, where it supplements other energy-saving systems, it is probably an effective addition.

Covering the roofs of the home and garage are RTS Standing Seam Shingles, made of 60 percent recycled steel. They have a lighter mass than alternative roofing products have, therefore, less structural support materials were needed. The lighter mass results in less retained heat and faster release of heat gained during the day.

The entry canopy roof is covered with Mirrorseal Roofing material, a saltwater-based material applied onto a polypropylene mesh. The product is known to have a high solar reflectance of 82 percent, more than three times greater than gravel-coat asphalt. Because of its reflectance, Mirrorseal Roofing material tends not to absorb heat from the sun as readily as other roofing materials.

The Peachtree exterior doors selected for the ESH are made of steel skins and polyurethane foam cores with thermally broken edges providing high insulation values of R-11 in the center of the doors. Attention has also focused on proper weatherstripping and thresholds to minimize air infiltration, lessening cooling energy needs.

The window systems, or fenestration, required much research to ensure energy savings. Fenestration comprises glass, glazings, and framing, all of which need to be considered. The choice of glazing materials can influence the quality of daylight within the house and its energy savings. The thermal properties of glass can affect both heating and cooling loads. The central design issues of glass for energy-efficient daylighting in hot arid climates are thermal conductivity (the rate at which heat is gained or lost), light transmission (the amount of light allowed to pass through the glass), emissivity (the amount of heat absorbed by the glass and radiated into the interior or exterior space), and shading coefficients (the ability of a glazing system to transmit solar heat and light). The frames surrounding the glass, if not chosen or installed correctly, can allow heat transfer that can negate the thermal efficiency of the glass itself.

In environmental homes, windows take on importance as a means of saving energy after all the other measures of thermal envelope efficiency have been maximized. To have windows function as energy-saving design elements, it is important to consider their

Option A	▪ Reduce the window area in a home by 10 percent from 19 percent to 17 percent of the floor area. ▪ Use shade screens or glazing products with a low shading coefficient.
Results	Home energy use can be reduced by approximately 1,000 kWh, or 6 percent.
Option B	▪ Reduce the window area in a home by 10 percent, from 19 percent to 17 percent of the floor area. ▪ Use glazing products with a low shading coefficient (factory tinted, not shade screen). ▪ Use low-E coatings and thermal breaks.
Results	Home energy use can be reduced by approximately 1,500 kWh, or 10 percent.

7. Relationship of fenestration and energy savings: two options

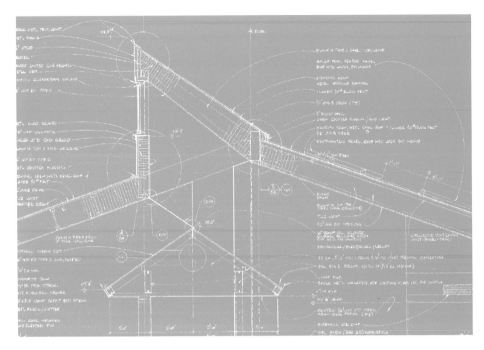

**Cross section showing
clerestory windows and
mechanical plenum/
daylight reflector**

orientation, their shading, their size relative to the floor space, and their actual performance characteristics. For the ESH, the decisions related to window design were based on various energy-use simulations that took into account window space, shading, and performance elements. Reducing window space while adding certain shading features results in reducing energy use for cooling and heating, as the options in table 7 illustrate.

As these two options suggest, simple measures, such as reducing window size by a small percentage and adding tinting or shade screens to produce a low shading coefficient, can result in effective savings in energy consumption. Window size and placement was an important factor in the plans for the home's energy requirements. As a percentage, windows account for approximately 17 percent of the ESH floor area, compared to 18 to 25 percent for standard homes of similar size.

The danger in simply reducing window size to conserve energy is to produce a dark, cavelike home that is unappealing to home buyers. The ESH integrates aesthetics with energy reduction: it allows in natural light while

reducing heat gain. The project team selected all the windows and glass systems to maximize the benefits from natural daylighting and offset the need for electrical lighting during the day, while protecting the house from detrimental heat gains. Natural light is enhanced by the patio door (facing south) and the clerestory windows that run along the north side of the house. The clerestory windows are shaded by 8-foot exterior fabric shades to prevent heat gain, and light is introduced throughout the home through the specially built reflective spline. Glass throughout is shaded by overhangs, awnings, and walls.

The windows used in the ESH are high-performance units encased by aluminum-clad wood frames. The aluminum-clad wood creates a "thermal break" that minimizes heat gain to the home's interior through the window frame. All the lower windows except the clerestory use a high-performance glazing system made up of a 1/8-inch-thick tempered gray-tinted outer pane and a 1/8-inch-thick tempered clear inner pane with a low-emissivity coating. The gray tint was chosen to reduce reflected heat gain and cut glare. These panes are separated by a 3/4-inch space filled with argon gas in which two sheets of low-emission film (Heat Mirror) are suspended. This gives the glass a low shading coefficient of 0.40, a visible light transmittance of 43 percent, and an R-value of 9, as defined by the National Fenestration Rating Council. At these values, the entire system allows only two-thirds of the heat gain or loss of typical double-paned windows and one-third of the heat gain or loss of a single-paned window. The glass keeps out heat or cold almost as well as a wall does in a typical older home.

The clerestory windows, which face north and are well shaded, do not experience direct heat gain. Because the purpose of the clerestory is to bring in as much light as possible while blocking heat transfer, these windows have the same glazing configuration as the rest of the windows in the home, but the clerestory windows have a clear outer pane, permitting 62 percent transmittance of visible light. This configuration still retains a shading coefficient of 0.52.

The patio door is a 1-inch-thick insulated glazing system with two panes separated by a single heat mirror film suspended in an argon gas fill. Like the windows, this glass system also has a

Interior, with daylight entering through clerestory windows

Energy-saving window

Coming Full Circle

The Environmental Showcase Home is showing us how we have come full circle in our energy use. Earliest humans used the sun directly for light and to provide the resources essential to survival. Later, as they began to use and control fire, they migrated into Europe, the Middle East, Asia, and the western hemisphere. For thousands of years, their only fuel was wood. It was a dispersed energy resource and there was a lot of it.

By 1650 the population had grown to five hundred million, and the forests that had once covered Europe were largely gone. The invention of a reliable water pump initiated the transition from wood to coal and launched the Industrial Revolution.

The nineteenth century witnessed a continued growth in the use of coal, and it was coal that powered the unprecedented increase in living standards. But the use of coal produced suffocating air pollution and it was bulky and hazardous to mine. By 1930, there were two billion people in the world, and a new transition was imminent, the move to oil.

The first oil well was drilled in western Pennsylvania in 1859, and this was followed soon after by great finds at Baku, west Texas, Indonesia, and elsewhere. By 1939, oil was considered the resource of the future. There were about three billion people in the world, and the peak of oil production was less than three decades away.

Now, as we approach the twenty-first century, we are still dependent upon oil, but we passed our peak in production in 1970 and we will pass the peak worldwide by 2020. As the world population nears six billion, what are our plans for the future? Two resources come to mind. The Environmental Showcase Home is showing us how to tap into the "resource of efficiency," a temporary resource created by the inefficiencies of the past. The Showcase Home, using a design that works with the local environment, is demonstrating perhaps the most important and compatible resource of all. We are coming full circle back to the energy source that fueled us ten thousand years ago—the sun.

Martin Pasqualetti
Professor of Geography
Arizona State University

high insulative value of R-8.3, a light transmittance rating of 57 percent, and a shading coefficient of about 0.36. This outstanding performance rating results from the green (Solex) tinted outer pane, a clear inner pane with a low-E coating, and the Heat Mirror film and argon gas within. This configuration results in the highest daylighting efficiency available in a production glazing system. The frame for the patio door is made of simple aluminum components, but because of the size of the doors, it becomes thermally insignificant in the overall heat transfer.

The garage's windows provide a less expensive option. They are designed to minimize heat transfer through the window frame by a continuous bead of low-conductivity material that thermally separates the exterior aluminum portion of the window frame from the interior portion. The windows are glazed with a gray-tinted outer pane. They also have a clear inner pane with a low-emissivity (low-E) coating and are filled with argon gas. This is a "standard optional" insulated glass package available from the window manufacturer. This glass has an R-3 insulation factor in its center, and the whole window has an R-value of 2.4.

Recycled aluminum is used to manufacture the window frames, and they are fully recyclable should they need to be removed or replaced.

ESH Total Energy Savings

The ESH demonstrates a variety of energy-saving ideas in both passive and active energy use. Passive energy design concepts include the home's east-west axis that minimizes sunlight exposure on its east and west walls. A smaller overall window area minimizes direct solar penetration. Proper shading of the home's windows and walls, insulation, and control of air filtration provide substantial energy savings. Active energy systems include energy-efficient systems for space heating and cooling, water heating, home appliances, and active solar energy technologies. Each individual appliance or technology in the ESH has the potential to save energy, but when the various elements are considered as a part of a system, the total energy savings become substantial.

The various energy technologies in the ESH and their savings have been analyzed by an energy-impact computer

Energy system	Features	Savings (kWh)
Space conditioning	Nordyne PowerMiser (SEER 20) heating, ventilating, and air conditioning system (HVAC) with water-heating function	3100
	Trane Super Efficiency heat pump system	1800
Electric hot water options	EPRI E-Tech heat pump water heater	1600
	Integrated heat pump with space conditioning (Nordyne PowerMiser)	1970
Lighting	Fluorescents and halogens	650
Energy-efficient appliances	Refrigerator, clothes washer, dishwasher, etc.	770
Solar technologies	Copper Cricket solar water heater and 2.7 kW of Solarex photovoltaic panels	3000

8. Energy savings in the ESH

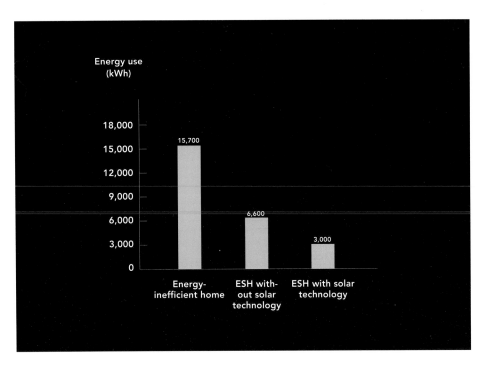

Energy use (kWh)

18,000
15,000
12,000
9,000
6,000
3,000
0

15,700

6,600

3,000

Energy-inefficient home

ESH without solar technology

ESH with solar technology

9. Energy use comparison

simulation assessment conducted by Energy Simulation Specialists of Arizona and are summarized in table 8. With the installation of the four key elements of energy use (the HVAC, the heat pump water heater, the energy-efficient appliances, and the lighting fixtures), together with the home's passive energy design, the ESH is estimated to reduce electricity use by 60 percent over an energy-inefficient home of similar size. When the solar technologies (solar water heating and photovoltaics) are included, then the ESH is estimated to use only *20 percent* of the energy of a typical energy-inefficient home.

Figure 9 displays the energy consumption in kWh for three different styles of home: the first is an energy-inefficient home, the next is the ESH if it had been built without solar technology, and the last is the ESH as it is built, with solar technology. The first home, approximately 2,000 square feet in size and occupied by three people, would use just under 16,000 kWh. The ESH, even without solar technology applications, would use only 6,600 kWh, saving around 60 percent over the energy-inefficient home. Incorporating solar technologies into the ESH significantly lessens total energy use to around 80 percent over the energy-inefficient home. If new homes were built using only *some* of these energy-saving technologies, the decrease in energy demand would be considerable.

By using as many of these technologies as possible in new and existing homes, we will be able to move that much closer to living within our resource means in the desert.

Sources

Anderson, Mary R. and Ronald J. Balon. 1983. *Solar Water Heating for Arizona Homes*. Phoenix, AZ: Arizona Solar Energy Commission.

Arizona Department of Commerce Energy Office. 1993. "AzHERS: A Rating System That Makes a Difference." *Arizona Energy News*. 6.

———. 1994. *Arizona Energy Data Quarterly Report, Third Quarter 1993*. Phoenix, AZ.

———. *Arizona Energy Patterns and Trends, 1960–1990*. Phoenix, AZ.

———. 1990. "Passive Solar Design." *Bright Ideas*. 1–3.

———. 1990. "Photovoltaics in Arizona." *Bright Ideas*. 1–3.

———. 1992. "Photovoltaics: Solar Electricity." *Bright Ideas*. 1–11.

Brown, Lester R., ed. 1994. *State of the World: 1994*. New York: W. W. Norton & Company.

Brown, Lester R., Hal Kane, and Ed Ayres. 1993. *Vital Signs 1992: The Trends That Are Shaping Our Future*. New York: W. W. Norton & Company.

Brown, Lester R., Hal Kane, and David M. Roodman. 1994. *Vital Signs 1993: The Trends That Are Shaping Our Future*. New York: W. W. Norton & Company.

Claman, Victor N. 1983. *How to Reduce Energy Costs in Your Building*. Boston, MA: Center for Energy Sharing.

Edison Electric Institute. 1991. *Statistical Yearbook of the Electric Utility Industry, 1990*. Washington, DC.

Flavin, Christopher, and Nicholas Lenssen. 1994. *Powering the Future: Blueprint for a Sustainable Electricity Industry*. Washington, DC: Worldwatch Institute.

Harms, Valerie. 1994. *Almanac of the Environment: The Ecology of Everyday Life*. New York: Grosset/Putnam, for the National Audubon Society.

Hayes, Dennis. 1992. "Keynote." *Energy, Environment & Architecture*. Washington, DC: The American Institute of Architects.

Lepley, Tom. 1993. Correspondence to APS Distribution Group Concerning Tilt Angle of PV Array for Environmental Showcase Home. October.

———. 1993. *Environmental Showcase Home: Solar Technology Recommendations*. Report to APS.

Loken, Steve, Walter Spurling, and Carol Price. 1993. *Guide to Resource Efficient Building Elements*. Missoula, MT: Center for Resourceful Building Technology.

"Newslog." 1994. IEEE *Spectrum*. March: 1.

"Newslog." 1994. IEEE *Spectrum*. June: 1.

U.S. Department of Energy. 1992. *State Energy Data Report, 1992: Consumption Estimates*. Washington, DC: Government Printing Office.

———. 1993. *State Energy Price and Expenditure Report, 1991*. Washington, DC: Government Printing Office.

World Resources Institute. 1993. *The 1994 Information Please Environmental Almanac*. Boston, MA: Houghton Mifflin Company.

3

Water Conservation

Water is the ultimate recyclable material: it evaporates into the atmosphere only to return as rain to the earth's surface, where it gathers into streams, rivers, and lakes, and replenishes groundwater. Water is also a limited resource: the water cycle only replenishes a given amount in any location, and although water is the most abundant chemical substance on the earth's crust, only 3 percent is fresh water available for our needs. As the world's population has grown, the relative share of the earth's fresh water supply has decreased on a per-person basis. According to the Worldwatch Institute, twenty-six countries whose combined population is 230 million have water supplies already inadequate to meet the needs of a moderately developed society—and populations are growing the fastest in some of the countries with the most severe water shortages.

In the United States, pollution has placed additional stress on our water resources. Approximately one-third of our river miles do not meet government water quality standards, with much of the water supply containing fertilizers, pesticides, chemical wastes, and by-products from mining operations. Even our rainfall is often contaminated with sulfur dioxide or nitrogen oxide from industrial and transportation sources.

Today we find ourselves dependent on a water supply that is being systematically depleted and mismanaged. This is particularly dangerous as we consume water from aquifers, the underground

Opposite page:
PVC pipes

reservoirs that have held water for centuries. The depletion of groundwater is an especially critical area of concern in Arizona, and the state government has implemented water management strategies to address the problem in the major metropolitan areas.

According to the Worldwatch Institute, about half of the U.S. population relies on groundwater supplies for its source of potable (drinking) water. Yet in states like Oklahoma, Texas, Arizona, and New Mexico, water is being withdrawn from wells and aquifers at rates exceeding replenishment. Overuse of water supplies from rivers and lakes adversely affects fish and wildlife habitats and the quality of surface water. The overuse of water also adds to environmental burdens in other areas, especially in the consumption of energy. Energy in the form of electricity, gasoline, or natural gas must be consumed in order to treat and pump water to meet the growing demand.

The United States is second only to Australia in per capita water use for municipal purposes (defined as residential and city service use, such as fire fighting and street cleaning). In the United States, we consume an average of 159 gallons of water per person every day—more than twice as much water per person as in the United Kingdom, four times more water per person than in Switzerland and Israel, and almost ten times as much as in China. Households account for about 57 percent of municipal water use in the United States.

These statistics show that we have not yet recognized the need for effective water management. Many cities and states, such as Tacoma, Washington, where water usage is 691 gallons per person per day, have not felt the pressures of scarce water and continue to use it without concern for the future. Typically, state and local governments use conservation measures as a short-term means of fighting drought, as was done recently in California. Long-term strategies for conserving water are just now being recognized in states where water is most scarce. Yet, a recent study estimates that 45 percent of Americans will live in areas with mandated water rationing by the end of the 1990s.

The city of Tucson, Arizona, which depends on groundwater for most of its water needs, may be considered a success story in municipal water conservation. In the late 1970s, Tucson was pumping water out of the ground at five times the rate it was being replenished. Tucson did several things to counteract the growing water supply problem. First, the city raised the price of water; second, it used public education to encourage the installation of household water-saving fixtures; and finally, it encouraged the replacement of grass lawns with desert landscaping. These efforts led to a 24 percent drop in per capita water use.

Other Arizona residents have not yet felt the urgency that Tucson residents felt about the scarcity of water. Eleven percent of our surface water (nearly 500 billion gallons) comes from the Colorado River, which supplies water to the southwestern United States. Scientists are now studying the negative effects of lowering the water level of the river on its fish, wildlife, and ecosystems. Annually, we are using 14 percent more of the state's groundwater than is replenished. Arizona ranks fifteenth in the nation in per capita water use, largely as a result of its extensive agricultural base. In Arizona, agriculture uses 76.5 percent of our water, municipalities use 16.3 percent, and industry consumes just 7.2 percent. As our land slowly becomes urbanized, it may become critical that we expand water management measures in the urban sector.

Water Conservation and Building Design

One way to conserve water is to incorporate water management strategies into building design. In the desert, the environment imposes a natural mandate on how we should build in order to conserve water. We should store rainwater, use native and low-water-use plants in our landscaping, and install the most effective water-saving devices in our homes. Simply replacing lawns with low-water-use plants can have a great effect on water conservation.

The *Design Issues Guide*, developed for the Environmental Showcase Home by the Center for Resourceful Building Technology and EcoGroup, Inc., emphasizes water conservation as one of the home's principal objectives:

With the increased prevalence of droughts and water shortages in the southwestern United States, water-use restrictions have been mandated to address critical water shortage situations. Concurrent with these "reactive" measures, many municipalities have instituted water conservation ordinances as a preventive way to limit the use of scarce fresh water supplies. Phoenix is one local municipality that has instituted an ordinance regarding low-water-use devices in new home construction [1980 code]. However, with a population that is expected to increase by 150 percent in the next 50 years, and considering the Phoenix groundwater table level has decreased by over 120 feet in the past 30 to 40 years, there needs to be more aggressive measures than are currently mandated in local ordinances to conserve the use of water. The Environmental Showcase Home should demonstrate some of the most water-conserving strategies in its design and use of available technologies.

The goal for the ESH was to reduce indoor and outdoor water use by 50 percent, compared to that of a typical production home in the Phoenix area, by using the following methods:

1. Demand reduction, which involves limiting the use of water through the installation of low-flow fixtures, low-water-use landscapes, and evaporation-limiting devices for irrigation.
2. Water management, which involves controlling water demand through use patterns that minimize need. For example, a sensor system can accomplish precise irrigation control by monitoring environmental conditions on a daily and seasonal basis before determining a watering schedule.
3. Rainwater harvesting, which is a simple process that gathers rainfall into a storage basin (cistern), where it is stored for later use for landscape irrigation.
4. Gray water reuse, which takes the gray water from such locations as bathtubs and laundry rooms and uses it on the landscape. Gray water from a family of four, together with rainwater harvesting, may produce enough water for a home's total landscape needs.

The indoor conservation measures incorporated into the ESH include water-saving shower heads and faucets, low-water-use appliances, and a gray water reuse system. Outdoor water conservation measures include a subsurface irrigation system, environmental monitoring and irrigation control devices, rainwater harvesting, and xeriscaping.

Fixture/Appliance	Typical production home Water rate	ESH Water rate	Typical production home Gallons/year (thousand)	ESH Gallons/year (thousand)
Toilet	3.5 gal/flush x 4 flushes/cap/day	1.5 gal/flush x 4 flushes/cap/day	20.4	8.8
Shower	3 gal/min x 4.6 min/cap/day	2.25 gal/min x 4.6 min/cap/day	20.2	15.1
Washing machine	55 gal/load x 0.3 loads/cap/day	Variable load. Mean load 20 gal/load x 0.3 loads/cap/day	24.1	8.7
Dishwasher	14 gal/load x 0.17 loads/cap/day	10 gal/load x 0.17 loads/cap/day	3.5	2.5
Faucet	8 gal/cap/day	4 gal/cap/day	11.7	5.8
Bath	50 gal/bath x 0.14 baths/cap/day	50 gal/bath x 0.14 baths/cap/day	10.2	10.2
Total indoor water use			90.1	51.1

10. Comparison of indoor water use by appliance

Water Savings

Table 10 shows the amount of indoor water consumed by four persons in one year in a typical production home in Phoenix and in the ESH. The comparison assumes similar floor space (2,000 square feet) and yard area for both homes. The amount of water estimated to be consumed in the ESH shows significant savings in indoor water use. Every year, a typical household in Phoenix is estimated to consume over 90,000 gallons of indoor water. In contrast, the yearly consumption of indoor water in the ESH is projected at 51,000 gallons—a reduction of 43 percent in indoor water use alone.

Outdoor water use, primarily for irrigation, accounts for a substantial percentage of the total residential use of water in Phoenix. A typical 2,000-square-foot turf landscape with above-ground irrigation requires approximately 58,000 gallons of water yearly. In contrast, a xeriscape area of equal size may use around 20,000 gallons of water every year, and even less after the first twelve to twenty-four months, the usual time it takes for new plants to become fully established.

Because of the water savings, the ESH landscape is predominantly xeriscape. The small amount of turf, or grass lawn, on the ESH site should be no larger than can be sustained by the amount of gray water generated by the home's eventual occupants. In the long term, no municipal water will be necessary for maintaining the lawn area, causing a significant savings in water use.

Even without an operational gray water system, the ESH is estimated to save 52 percent of the indoor and outdoor water used by a typical Phoenix residence (figure 11). If the potential of using gray water for irrigation is eventually realized, the water savings will be even greater.

Indoor Water Systems

The ESH project team chose many products for the home based on their ability to conserve water, including low-flow fixtures and water-saving devices in sinks, shower heads, toilets, clothes washer, and dishwasher.

The ESH contains separate bathrooms for the master suite, the children's room, and the guest suite, providing the opportunity to demonstrate various brands of shower heads and other bathroom fixtures. The master suite bathroom is equipped with the Incredible Head shower head, produced by Resources Conservation, Inc., of Connecticut. This new low-flow head, made of solid brass, is designed to exceed the new 1994 EPA water conservation regulations (prescribing a flow rate of 2.25 gallons per minute). In addition, the Incredible Head has a unique on/off switch that allows the user to turn off the water flow anytime during the showering process, conserving both water and the energy needed to heat the water. The flow rate can save around 50 percent of a typical shower's water consumption. This bathroom also features a low-water-use toilet (1.6 gallons or less

per flush). Manufactured by Kohler, the Rialto Pressure Lite toilet contains a pressure-assisted flushing mechanism and cleaning mechanism to assure an adequate flush with a minimum amount of water.

The children's bathroom features a Chatham shower head, manufactured in Edison, New Jersey. Rated number one in the nation by *Consumer Reports* magazine, the Chatham head meets the 1994 water conservation regulations and also allows individual adjustment of the water flow. Made from forged brass, the Chatham head allows the adjustment of spray patterns from a needle shower to a heavy wash.

The toilet in this bathroom is the Briggs Ultra-Conserver, a gravity-fed siphon action toilet that uses less than 1.5 gallons of water per flush. A companion "toilet lid sink," located above the reduced-size toilet tank, is for hand washing. When the toilet is flushed, clean water is routed through the gooseneck spigot in the sink. After it is used to wash hands, the water then drains into the tank and bowl to be used in the next flush.

The guest bathroom has an Alsons shower head, a low-water-flow fixture.

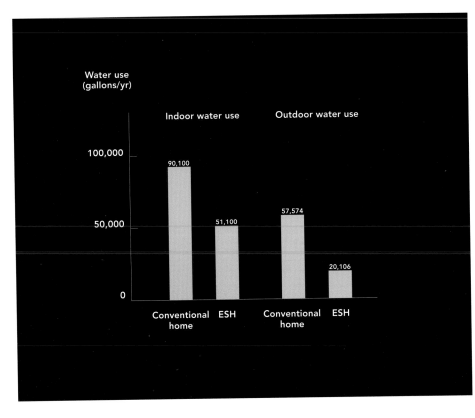

**11. Water use
comparison**

This shower head is hand-held or mounted on an adjustable bar for better access by the elderly and disabled.

The guest bathroom also includes the Fluidizer, an extremely low-flush toilet (0.6 gallons per flush) manufactured by Control Fluidics of Greenwich, Connecticut, which has field-tested the unit for nine years. The toilet utilizes hydraulic attrition to break up waste products into small particles, providing adequate flushing while lightening the load on waste treatment plants.

All faucets in the ESH have aerators that allow flows of only 2.5 gallons per minute in the kitchen and 1.5 gallons per minute in the bathrooms. The washing machine (model LT350R by White-Westinghouse) is a front-loading, variable-load washer with a mean load of 20 gallons. Its estimated annual use of 8,700 gallons per year is much lower than the 24,100 gallons per year used by a typical water-inefficient machine. Because using less water to wash a load of clothes requires less heated water, this machine also uses less energy. The dishwasher (Amana DU7500) is designed to save approximately 1,000 gallons of water and 250 kWh in energy per year over standard equipment.

The Pool

The home planners debated extensively over whether to build a pool. Some who were against a pool viewed it as a water-consuming rather than a water-conserving feature. The others who advocated a pool convinced the group that the ESH could *demonstrate* ways in which a pool can be more environmentally responsible, thus diminishing the impact of something that is likely to remain a dominant feature of home building in Phoenix.

The architect, Edward Jones, had originally conceived the pool as multifunctional, providing support for other environmental design elements of the home. Early in the design process, he proposed a sunken garden/family play area to the side of and under the house. To reduce summer heat in the outdoor play area, water would cascade down from the pool (which would be at a higher elevation) and a fan would direct water-cooled air throughout the subsurface play area, much like an evaporative cooler. The plan also called for a special emergency system that would pump pool water in case of a fire. The project team, however, decided to forego the sunken garden plan because it would not be easily transferable to production homebuilding.

Although the best environmental option is to have no pool, the project team decided to go ahead with a small play pool to acknowledge lifestyle considerations and the demands of the home-buying public. They believed that showcasing efficient choices for constructing and maintaining a pool would help encourage better use of the water and energy resources it needed.

Several environmental features were incorporated into the pool system. The pump, manufactured by Hayward Pool Products, has a two-speed motor that is estimated to reduce energy use by about 30 percent. The 1.5 horsepower setting is used for vacuuming and heavy cleaning for about two hours out of an assumed eight-hour running time, and the 0.25 horsepower setting is used for general cleaning, thus saving energy during the overall cycle. While standard motors are about 64 percent energy-efficient, the Hayward Super II has been established at 79 percent. Greater efficiency in pool motors has other benefits in addition to reduced energy use, including better filtration, which extends

the life of pool systems, and cleaner pools, which decrease water use because they need to be drained and refilled less often. Another feature of the pool system is that the pump's diatomaceous earth filter is designed in such a way as to allow 300 gallons of backwash water to reenter the pool through a secondary filter instead of being drained off and wasted.

The Challenger 3000 Ionization System demonstrates an effective alternative to using chlorine to purify water. An electrode-sensing device monitors water conditions and releases copper ions into the water when required. The resulting reactions eliminate bacteria, algae, and excessive minerals from the water. This sanitation system is environmentally beneficial because it purifies the water with fewer toxic chemicals and provides chlorine-free swimming.

The Heliocol solar pool heating system circulates water between the main pool pump and six solar collector panels on the roof. As water rises through collector tubes, it is heated by the sun and returned to the pool. Because the system uses free energy from the sun, it is the most environmentally responsible option for heating pool water.

Outdoor living area with pool

Rainwater harvesting system

Although some manufactured energy is required for pumping pool water through riser tubes to the collector, the Heliocol system is designed to lower head pressure and keep pumping requirements to a minimum. The heating extends the pool season by as much as three to four months, providing better use of the pool and its water.

The Save-T Cover automatic pool cover, made of laminated vinyl with a mechanical glider, provides both an effective thermal covering and a safety factor. This particular cover is powered by a photovoltaic panel and a battery generator system. Pool covers decrease the rate of evaporation, reducing the need to refill with fresh water by as much as 30 to 50 percent. They can also increase water temperature by 10 to 15 degrees, extending the swimming season and reducing energy demands on pool heaters.

The pool is a problematic feature of an environmental home. In spite of its energy-saving features, more could have been done to integrate the pool into the home's systems. The early design, which had called for the pool water to be part of an outdoor cooling system and a fire protection system, would have helped justify the choice to build the pool. These features would have added to its current role as an educational item.

Water Harvesting

Rainwater Harvesting

The ESH demonstrates two rainwater harvesting systems. One captures rainfall at each corner of the home. Rain hitting the pitched roof surface flows along two gutters and is guided to four grated cement slabs on the ground that lead to the catch basins. The rainwater flows to a single tank made from recycled plastic. Also flowing to this tank is gray water generated from the low-flow showers, tubs, sinks, and the clothes washer. The rainwater/gray water from the tank can irrigate the landscape through an automated subsurface drip irrigation system. If the storage tank nears capacity, overflow can be directed as irrigation to the landscaped areas.

A second rainwater harvesting system begins on the "butterfly" roof on the garage. A central gutter collects rainwater, causing it to flow directly into an aboveground cistern located on the east side of the garage. Water from the cistern can be directed manually to the vegetable garden east of the garage.

Rain that falls on the landscape is collected in retention basins designed into the landscape forms, minimizing runoff into the storm sewer system. The site is designed to capture rainwater: hard surfaces generally are sloped toward adjacent plant areas, and there are several bermed areas and mounds that facilitate rainwater catchment. The west side of the home has a significant catchment area, and the garden area is contoured for rainwater catchment and flood irrigation during periods of water oversupply.

Gray Water

The use of a gray water system for the ESH was recommended by the *Design Issues Guide* and by the Land Use and Water Conservation work group (composed of various project design team members) who noted that gray water reuse for residential landscapes is almost nonexistent, unless part of a city service. The group recommended that the home pioneer such a system by having a separate reservoir for capturing, holding, and distributing both rainwater and gray water on a timed basis. The captured water was intended for high-water-use landscape areas such as turf, so that minimal potable water would be used on them.

Following these recommendations, the project team planned to use a gray water system in the ESH, but found that ADEQ and Maricopa County forbid the use of gray water systems in the county because of potential health problems. Through discussions with the agencies, APS was able to secure a construction-only permit because the ESH will be without a live-in family to generate gray water for the first three years. When APS sells the home, the new owners will be able to apply for an operating permit for the system.

The gray water system was designed, manufactured, and installed by AGWA Systems of California. The piping system prevents inadvertent mixing of gray water with any rainwater that may over-flow the rainwater collection units, which could release gray water above ground. With the subsurface irrigation system, the gray water will remain below ground, significantly reducing potential problems. To further avoid potential problems, a valve and timer have been

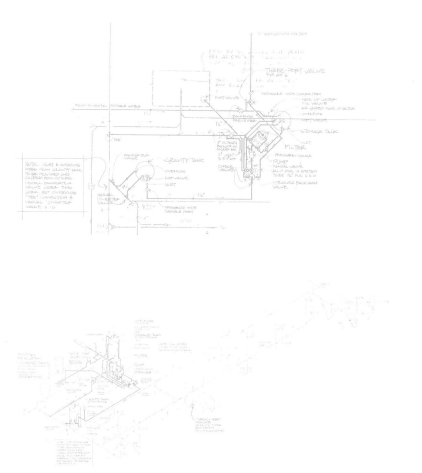

Diagrams for gray water installation

added to the washing machine pipes so that the water of certain loads such as diapers can go to the sewer instead of entering the gray water system. Figure 12 shows how the AGWA gray water system works.

AGWA Systems personnel estimate that about 65 percent of indoor household water use produces gray water. Based on their experience in California, they estimate that each household of four persons in a non-water-conserving home can produce about 1,650 gallons of gray water per week, enough to support a yard consisting of 900 square feet of lawn, several mature shade or fruit trees, and 15 large shrubs. The abundance of nutrients in gray water also makes it feasible for sustaining ground covers, lawns, and shrubs. The reused water filters through the soil to recharge groundwater supplies.

One analysis shows that 126 gallons per day of gray water can be generated by the ESH, but the amounts would vary depending on the water-conserving behavior of the members of the household. This amount of gray water would exceed the irrigation needs of the small turf area on the ESH lot. These figures suggest the far-reaching environmental implications if gray water systems were added to the new homes built in the Phoenix area.

The system occupies a 5-by-7-foot area of the lot. The gray water gravity tank has a 55-gallon capacity and is sized to accommodate a simultaneous one-minute discharge of a full bathtub, a laundry sink, and two lavatories. The pump can distribute the gray water at a rate of 45 to 55 gallons per minute; if it fails or is delayed, a strainer and filtering system will automatically backwash into the city sewer system. The rainwater/gray water storage tank holds 500 gallons, a size that would accommodate two days of maximum house flow, or four days of average flows.

Irrigation Systems

The AGWA Systems gray water storage unit is linked to the ROOTGUARD system, a subsurface drip irrigation system manufactured by Geoflow, Inc. An underground drip system follows the same design principles as surface drip irrigation systems but supplies irrigation at the root zone, eliminating many common surface irrigation problems such as water flowing away from the vegetation, pooling water, and evaporation.

Made from durable polyolefins, parallel drip-lines (about 12 to 14 inches apart) are buried 6 to 8 inches below ground and are connected by the PVC (plastic) pipe to the gray water-recycling system. ROOTGUARD is designed to protect itself for approximately twenty years from plant roots intruding and clogging the system, by means of a special inhibiting agent called TREEFLAN, which creates a barrier around the emitters (water outlets).

The ROOTGUARD system prevents evaporation and runoff and is easy to install, even in narrow or odd-shaped areas. Among the many benefits of an underground irrigation system are the aesthetics of an invisible system, a decrease in vandalism or other damage that sometimes occurs with aboveground parts, and reduced owner liability by eliminating the causes of injury from wet surfaces. The only exception to the subsurface irrigation system is the aboveground rainwater cistern that delivers water to the vegetable garden.

The AGWA gray water retrieval and the ROOTGUARD irrigation system are monitored and controlled by a special "user-friendly" computer program called Calsense. Besides controlling all

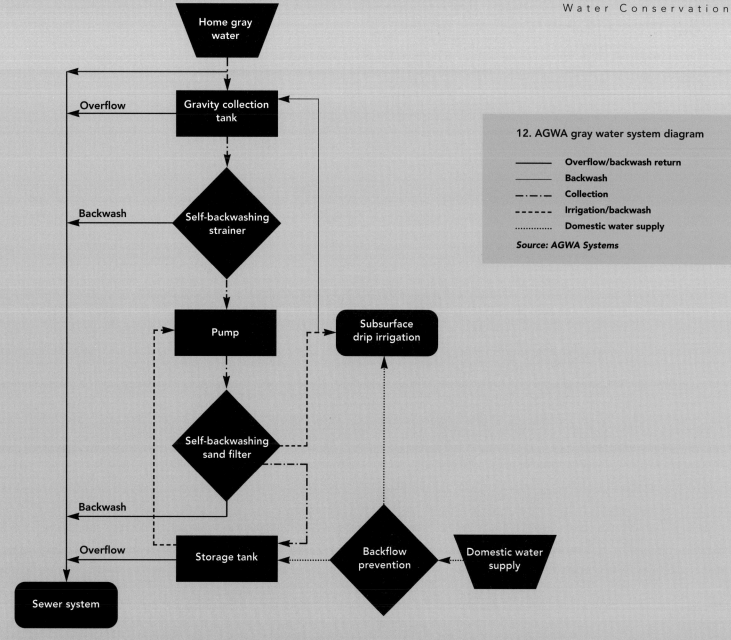

12. AGWA gray water system diagram

—————— Overflow/backwash return
———— Backwash
—·—·— Collection
------- Irrigation/backwash
············· Domestic water supply

Source: AGWA Systems

Landscape design

the irrigation system components used in the ESH, the Calsense allows the homeowner to program adjustable cycles and soak periods for each station and design timed programs for daily, weekly, seasonal, or climatic changes. The program generates water use data by month and year, allowing the user to input annual water budget plans that the system then monitors for compliance. The system is automated and can adjust water use whenever over-budget conditions occur and can shut down single stations automatically without shutting down the total system.

The Landscape Design

Early in the idea stage of the ESH, a team of landscape and water experts came together to develop criteria for the site and landscape design. The team consisted of Ray McNulty, a mechanical engineer; Jeff Shively of the Arizona Department of Commerce Energy Office; Gary Swindler of Eco-Group, Inc.; Ron Mark, a water landscape expert from Xeris Group; Bob Munari, Arizona Department of Environmental Quality; Tom Hahn, project technical architect from Jones Studio, Inc.; and Robert Thompson, the home's principal landscape architect. The team evaluated the site issues and established a set of design criteria and generic principles that can be applied to any site. The method used by the team to evaluate concepts and items for selection in the ESH site and landscape design was based on a weighted system of criteria and on the xeriscape principles shown in table 13.

One of the team's initial concerns was to avoid the loss of the site's native plants. In Phoenix home developments, the sites are often cleared of all plant life, resulting in significant losses in native plant materials and a change in the sites' original character. Based on recent trends to preserve major vegetation and important site features, the team members argued strongly for keeping significant native plants at the ESH site through sensitive site design. The final lot selected, however, was barren of any native plants; therefore, the policy was not applicable.

Other landscape design recommendations were based on a preservation/ conservation philosophy. The following guidelines were established:

1. Maximize the use of drought-tolerant plants
2. Use plants that, when mature, will not depend on a regular supply of potable water
3. Collect rainfall to water plants for appropriate areas of the yard
4. Design the environment to provide maximum shade or sun where most beneficial

The goal of the landscaping design is to irrigate all the plant material on the property without using potable municipal water by applying the principles of xeriscape design. The plant material selected, representing a wide variety of native plants, is consistent with the approved list of drought-tolerant plants from the Arizona Department of Water Resources (ADWR).

These plants can usually survive on seasonal rain alone, but the design will use supplemental water for the first twelve to twenty-four months (especially during summer months) to help the plants stabilize. Once the plants have stabilized, the plan is to eliminate potable water for their irrigation. However, this plan to use supplemental water has been criticized by several local botanists. They claim that the extra

Planning and design

A properly planned xeriscape takes into account regional landscape requirements and existing vegetation.

Soil analysis

Soil amendments can improve soil moisture penetration and water-holding capacity.

Efficient irrigation

For efficient water use, irrigate turf areas separately from other plantings. Landscape plantings should also be grouped according to similar water needs. Trees, shrubs, flowers and groundcovers can be watered efficiently with low-volume drip, spray, or bubbler emitters. Water only when needed.

Practical turf areas

Locate turf in areas where it provides functional benefits. Turf is best separated from plantings of trees, shrubs, groundcovers, and flowering plants so that it may be irrigated separately. Turf can be replaced with other, less water-demanding materials.

Appropriate plant selection

It is important to place the right plant in the right place. Many trees, shrubs, and groundcovers that require little or no supplemental irrigation are readily available.

13. Xeriscape principles

Source: Adapted from Ewan (1992)

**Shaded outdoor
living area**

water is not necessary for drought-tolerant plants and that it will encourage the tops of the plants to develop at the expense of the roots. The botanists are concerned that when the water is reduced or turned off, the plants may not survive.

Another criticism of the landscape plan is that if the plants will not need supplemental water in the long term, then installing a gray water system in the ESH just to water its small turf area is an impractical and expensive solution. Its presence on the site is justified only to show how a gray water system would work if it were operational. However, such a system will only be transferable to other projects if homeowners choose to maintain a turf lawn and if they can obtain an operating permit.

Grass lawns do not fit any of the team's criteria. Turf requires constant application of water, provides no shade, and is not native to the desert. It requires extensive application of pesticides, herbicides, and fertilizers, and there are substantial costs related to its waste disposal (approximately 25 percent of landfill space in Phoenix is devoted to grass clippings and other yard waste).

The Land Use and Water Conservation work group was aware of these drawbacks. Despite its concerns, the group felt that some use of turf was necessary to provide a small recreation area. Their report states:

> Its size would be limited by the amount of harvested rainwater and gray water produced on-site. By limiting the turf to this volume, we can minimize the use of potable water for landscape irrigation. Turf could be used for functional or recreational needs if it could be justified by utilizing only reused water.

According to xeriscape criteria, turf areas should be limited to reduce water use. The ESH was designed with a very limited turf area relative to the total outdoor area and was placed close to the home. The purpose was to have a play area outdoors for children and pets and to provide an expansion of the indoor space to the outdoors. The location of the pool and turf area together on the south side of the house also tends to attenuate heat sink effects.

In the broadest sense, the Environmental Showcase Home, as its name suggests, exists to showcase various uses of systems and materials in building environmentally responsible homes. The use of turf is limited, but it is displayed in such a way as to educate the public on environmentally responsible approaches to turf (such as the use of nonherbicide applications, the use of gray water for irrigation, and underground irrigation).

The dominant plant palette of the ESH is the vegetation of the Sonoran Desert, including Palo Verde, Mesquite, Sweet Acacia, Desert Ironwood, and various cacti. The landscape is characterized as a drought-tolerant xeriscape with plants mostly native to the Central Arizona Basin and Range. Various shrubs include Texas Sage, Cassia Brittlebush, Creosote, and Red Sage, with accent shrubs of Desert Spoon, Red Yucca, and Agave. Cacti are used as accents near the high-visibility areas to provide a sculptured character to the landscape. Cacti varieties include the Saguaro, Ocotillo, Barrel, and Opuntia species.

The landscaped areas directly west of the house and the southeast corner will feature a number of large trees interspersed with shrubs and ground covers. The trees will reduce solar gain at low sun angles and help shade the home

from the summer's heat. The north and west sides of the house have low berms to provide a barrier between the home and streets. At the east and west ends of the home, surrounded by the plant materials, are two patios that provide pleasant microclimates for indoor/outdoor living. These shaded enclosed gardens serve to reduce the heating load at extremely low sun angles. The metal trellis slats over the patios are angled specifically to block all summer sun throughout the peak of the day, while allowing in maximum winter sun.

The planting design was also based on reducing solar heat gain during the summer season while allowing solar penetration during the cooler winter months. Gregory McPherson and Charles Sacamano argue that proper landscaping can be a significant factor in reducing energy costs.

Recent research shows that shade from just three trees located next to a typical ranch-style residence in Phoenix reduces the number of hours cooling is needed by 17 percent. . . . Watered shrubs can reduce a home's cooling requirements up to 24 percent, and a mature tree canopy can cut cooling costs up to 42 percent.

Metal louvers provide shade for outdoor living area *Background:* **detail of louver**

**Structure for
living fence**

Large desert trees located west and east of the home will protect its walls from maximum heat gain during the summer months. Fewer trees are planted on the home's southern exposure to permit heat gain from the lower solar angles of winter.

The area north of the home between the home and garage is devoted to a patio garden. This garden, an extension of the kitchen, is to be shaded and enclosed, yet open to natural ventilation and landscaped with lush plantings. It serves as the home's "oasis" on warmer days and evenings.

The northwest corner of the site, where Greenway Road and 60th Street meet, features a 36- to 40-inch-high berm, heavily planted with desert trees, including Palo Verdes and Mesquites interspersed with lower shrubs and ground cover. The berm was originally planned to be 5- to 6-feet high to make a visual statement and to serve as a noise barrier between the home and the streets. The team decided that a high berm would create a visual barrier and that a lower berm would maintain an open feeling around the home.

Running south and east of the bermed area is the driveway, consisting of stabilized decomposed granite. This native material is durable, retains porosity (water can readily move through it), and, because of its light color, reflects heat. Vegetation on both sides of the driveway provides shade.

A vegetable garden is planned for the area east of the garage. The garden area will be watered from the aboveground cistern containing rainwater from the garage roof.

Some of the landscape features of the home are not directly connected to the conservation of water, but serve other, more aesthetic, ends. For instance, a "living fence" has taken the place of block stucco fences that typically surround the back yards (and sometimes the front yards) of most production homes in Phoenix. The living wall, made of a wire fabric fence with vines growing on it, meanders along most of the boundary of the lot, providing a border to the property and an open natural look to the site. The snakelike form of the fence permits plant growth on both sides of the fence. The idea of the living fence is to move away from the straight-line block construction walls typical of the city and replace them with a more open, natural look.

Bob Thompson, landscape architect for the ESH, explained the team's feelings about the effect typical fencing patterns have on neighborhoods in the Phoenix area.

One of the things we absolutely all agreed about, was that one of the problems with the homes in the Phoenix metropolitan area is the block fence. From one house to the next, to the next, and the next—they're all fenced in with block. There's no openness; there's no sense of community; you can't talk to people.

We tried to establish early on the idea that there is no front yard, back yard, or side yard. The whole outdoors is basically usable space. The living fences were created because of Eddie's [Jones] concern about not putting up block fences all the way behind the house, separating back yard from front yard, if you will. The idea was to create a wall element—a wire fabric fence with vines growing on it. The wire fabric allows us to give the fence a serpentine form, and the vines growing along the fence will, over a period of time, give people the privacy that they're looking for. At the same time, it won't be like a block fence.

The amount and source of the water required to maintain the vines have not been determined. In this case, aesthetics may have won out over conservation.

Much attention was given to planning the landscape on the basis of "hydrozones," or areas of differing irrigation requirements. Plants with similar needs are grouped into hydrozones, reflecting small ecosystems in the landscape and requiring varying amounts of water. The landscaped area of the home will have around twenty-two areas broken into four or five hydrozones for meter supply purposes. A computer monitoring system will continually evaluate the moisture needs.

The ESH landscape design is consistent with the principles of hydrozone landscape planning, as described by Gregory McPherson and Charles Sacamano in *Southwestern Landscaping That Saves Energy and Water* (1989). The authors suggest landscape planning around four hydrozones. The "principal hydrozone" is an area that requires more water because the area is utilized more intensely for recreation or aesthetic reasons. In the ESH this hydrozone is represented by the small turf area. In the "secondary hydrozone," less water

The Conservation of Resources

In the Environmental Showcase Home, we have brought the concerns of product selection together with the economic reality of the marketplace. The outcome, we believe, is a balance of environmental and energy advancement that should be considered in today's Southwest homebuilding industry. While the ESH presents a host of features and technologies, its primary objective extends beyond those applications. Its true purpose is to educate home buyers and homebuilders about the availability of environmental and energy-saving products and the benefits of incorporating them into the marketplace. If we are successful in meeting that objective, the consumption of energy, water, natural resources, and materials will be significantly reduced, resulting in measurable environmental gains that will improve our quality of life.

Richard MacLean
Vice President, Environmental, Health and Safety Initiatives
Arizona Public Service

is used for plants that provide focal points in patio areas. The "minimal hydrozone" uses rainwater with some supplemental water, particularly during dry summer months and for young desert trees with fast growth rates. No additional water is required for the "elemental hydrozone," typified by cacti and other drought-tolerant plants with slow growth rates.

Environmental Benefits of Conserving Water

Using less water in our residences provides direct environmental benefits by reducing the depletion of surface water and groundwater and reducing the burden on municipalities to treat water and wastewater. A further, frequently overlooked, environmental benefit of using less water is energy savings. Pumping groundwater and surface water to reach residential customers requires substantial energy; residential water conservation translates into lower energy use, which in turn reduces demand for energy, thereby lowering the need to build more power plants. Reduced energy demands also result from having to heat less water for bathing and washing. The ESH, with its latest indoor water-saving technologies and creative landscape design and irrigation devices, addresses our need to save both water and energy and thus provides a more sustainable type of housing for the future.

Sources

Brown, Lester R., ed. 1994. *State of the World 1994*. New York: W.W. Norton & Company.

Brown, Lester R., Hal Kane, and Ed Ayres. 1993. *Vital Signs 1993: The Trends That Are Shaping Our Future*. New York: W.W. Norton & Company.

EcoGroup, Inc., and Center for Resourceful Building Technology. 1993. *Design Issues Guide*. Tempe, AZ.

Eden, Susanna, and Mary G. Wallace. 1992. *Arizona Water: Information and Issues*. Tucson, AZ: Water Resources Research Center, University of Arizona.

Ewan, Joseph. 1992. *Residential Landscapes for the Southwest*. Master's thesis, University of California, Berkeley.

Jenkins, V. S. 1994. *The Lawn: A History of an American Obsession*. Washington, DC: Smithsonian Institution Press.

Lyklema, J., and T.E.A. van Hylckama. 1988. "Water, Something Peculiar." In *Perspectives on Water, Uses and Abuses*, edited by David H. Speidel, Lon C. Ruedisili, and Allen F. Agnew. New York: Oxford University Press. 7–11.

McPherson, Gregory, and Charles Sacamano. 1989. *Southwestern Landscaping That Saves Energy and Water*. Tucson: University of Arizona Press.

Phoenix Building Safety Department. 1980. *City of Phoenix Construction Code*. Phoenix, AZ.

The 1994 Information Please Environmental Almanac. 1993. Boston: Houghton Mifflin.

Postel, Sandra. 1988. "The Consequences of Mismanagement." In *Perspectives on Water: Uses and Abuses*, edited by David H. Speidel, Lon C. Ruedisili, and Allen F. Agnew. New York: Oxford University Press. 307–25.

Rodgers, Peter P. 1988. "The Future of Water." In *Perspectives on Water, Uses and Abuses*, edited by David H. Speidel, Lon C. Ruedisili, and Allen F. Agnew. New York: Oxford University Press. 372–82.

Schultz, R. D. 1991. *Turn Off the Tap: How to Cut Your Water Use by 50%*. Albuquerque, NM: ECOTime.

Sheridan, David. 1988. "The Desert Blooms—at a Price." In *Perspectives on Water, Uses and Abuses*, edited by David H. Speidel, Lon C. Ruedisili, and Allen F. Agnew. New York: Oxford University Press. 251–69.

Thompson, Robert. Interview with David Pijawka. 20 July 1994.

4

Building Materials

The past few years have witnessed an increase in the number of environmentally friendly homebuilding materials available to the trade: there are carpets made of plastic bottles, insulation made of newspapers, lumber made of wood chips, and floor tiles made of windshield glass. Many manufacturers have begun using either pre- or postconsumer waste for their end products, while others have gone beyond simple recycling and have applied principles of resource efficiency to the entire process of manufacture.

There is a range of factors that goes into determining how environmentally friendly a product is and the selection of materials to meet all environmental goals is difficult.

It does little good to recycle materials if the resulting manufacturing process releases significant amounts of toxins into the atmosphere, nor does it help the environment if a "good" product has to be transported hundreds of miles, adding energy costs and air pollution to its byproducts.

This chapter examines the decision-making process that went into choosing resource- and energy-efficient materials for the Environmental Showcase Home and some of the trade-offs that had to be made. Surprising discoveries were made concerning the availability and quality of the products and the companies that made them, many of which led to even higher standards for the home than APS had originally envisioned. There is a groundswell of interest in the manufacture of environmental products

Opposite page:
Oriented strand board (OSB)

Energy efficiency

Energy-efficient production methods
Energy-efficient design
Energy-efficient usage

Sustainability

Recycled content
Recyclable
Sustainable source material and production process
Low maintenance and durable

Transferability

Cost-effectiveness
Availability
Acceptability

Health

Avoidance of harmful chemicals
Reduction of off-gassing

Qualities of supplier or manufacturer

Commitment to resource efficiency
In-house environmental programs
Marketing commitment to environmental responsibility
Local production capability

14. Factors considered in the choice of products and materials for the ESH

and materials for homebuilding, and both producers and consumers are becoming more aware of how their actions affect the environment.

Resource-Efficient Materials in the ESH

With the input of APS personnel and several technical advisors, Jones Studio chose the building materials for the ESH. The selection process was not always straightforward due to the many factors that had to be considered in each decision. In addition to factors such as the use of recycled materials for structural components, energy-efficient insulation qualities for wall and roof materials, and energy-saving features for appliances, the architects also considered the costs of the materials and their transport, the availability of the materials, as well as code compliance and other issues of the building trade. Trade-offs were necessary, for one product rarely met all the criteria. Products other than those chosen may have been resource- or energy-efficient, but perhaps were unavailable for the construction schedule, were inappropriate for the local climate, or were otherwise not compatible with this particular home design. Finally, ESH products and materials had to meet all minimum standards that had been set for the home. For instance, a product with high recycled content may not have been chosen because of potentially harmful chemicals used in its manufacture.

The major concepts that guided the choice of materials were energy efficiency, sustainability, transferability, health, and the environmental commitment of the manufacturer (table 14). The first of these, energy efficiency, refers first to energy savings in the product's manufacturing process. Some materials used in environmental homes, such as adobe blocks, rammed earth, straw bales, and stone, reflect very low input of energy. The goal in environmentally efficient building practices is to find materials that have not required an excessive amount of energy in their manufacture. Energy efficiency also refers to the fact that a product's use in the home must save energy. Therefore, its placement, function, and structural qualities must all combine to allow lower energy use than that of a comparable product.

Another issue, that of sustainability, includes the concept of resource efficiency. Sustainable materials are readily renewed in the environment, do not adversely affect the environment from which they come, and do not permanently deplete the resource or energy base that makes them possible. Wood is often held up as a sustainable product because trees can be regrown. Wood, however, may not be sustainable if it comes from the logging of old-growth forests. Sustainable practices must take into account all factors in a product's development and use, not just those that are convenient to measure.

Transferability was an important consideration. If a product is transferable, other builders are able to obtain it and use it without undue cost or difficulty. Because the ESH is intended to demonstrate environmentally sensitive ideas that could influence production home-building in the next three to five years, the materials chosen had to be transferable. The architects might have chosen to construct the home out of compressed straw bales (a currently available system) because that material met all of the criteria, but straw bales probably would not have been readily

accepted by either builders or buyers in the near future.

In the past, health has been overlooked as a criterion for the selection of materials for home construction. However, indoor air pollution, defined as harmful or hazardous materials in the air, is now recognized as a potential threat to health. A wide range of adverse health effects can be caused by even short-term exposure to these contaminants, and in acute cases prolonged exposure can cause serious health effects. With recent concerns about the effect of formaldehyde and other chemicals on indoor air quality, the design team chose to make this a primary consideration in its choice of materials, especially for interior finishes.

The final consideration in the selection of materials was the environmental commitment of the supplier, whose in-house management and marketing programs had to reflect an environmental sensibility. Because the construction of the ESH was to present a learning experience for other builders in the Valley, the project team felt that it should have the support of as many suppliers, providers, and manufacturers as possible to help spread the word.

Choice and Evaluation of Materials

Had the ESH been built five years ago, many of the resource-efficient materials that it uses would not have been available. Until recently, the market for resource-efficient building materials was quite poor. There were a few products that were widely used and available nationally. However, most environmentally responsible materials were in very limited use, made by small local companies with little recognition outside their immediate geographical areas. The current availability of a wide range of environmentally friendly products was a bonus for the ESH.

However, the very fact that so many products had become available in such a short time actually made it more difficult to make selections. Even during the construction phase of the ESH, there was a rapid proliferation of environmental products and new product development. This meant that the builders and designers underwent a continual learning process during the course of the project; sometimes decisions were postponed until the last minute in order that new developments

could be evaluated. All attempts were made to hold to the proposed building schedule but occasional delays could not be avoided.

With so many new materials to choose from, it became apparent that the environmental claims by the manufacturer needed to be validated. APS contracted with Science Certification Systems of Oakland, California, to review the environmental claims of the building materials and to analyze the major systems of the home: the roof, walls, and floors. In addition, experts from Arizona State University in the fields of energy, construction, and the environment were asked to evaluate the benefits of various energy- and water-conserving appliances and features.

Computer simulation modeling by Energy Simulation Specialists of Arizona and APS personnel helped determine what combination of features and materials would maximize energy efficiency. Through the modeling exercises, the project team was able to assess the various options for energy efficiency in the home and to see what the results would be in energy savings. Small changes in certain energy strategies, technologies, or materials were found to

have significant impacts on the reduction of energy. The modeling exercise proved to be a valuable tool in selecting various options.

Materials for the ESH

The architects changed their decisions often over the course of the project. In some cases they substituted a more available product for one less available, while in others they found that substituting a product or system required significant redesign. The following catalog of the systems of the ESH describes the primary materials used in each system and identifies the reason for their selection. Appendix B lists specific manufacturer information for the products used in the ESH.

Paving

Paving materials used for driveways and walkways can create several problems in the desert climate. Not only are impervious materials such as concrete and asphalt high in embodied energy, they absorb and trap heat, contributing substantially to the ever-increasing average daily temperature in Phoenix.

To solve these problems, the architects reduced concrete surface areas, eliminated all asphalt, used stabilized granite for hardscape elements, sited paved surfaces to the north and east of the home, and created shade on any paved surface wherever possible.

The driveways of the ESH are paved with crushed granite gravel stabilized with psyllium grain powder. When wetted, the granite hardens to nearly the density of asphalt. It does not soften when wet, yet allows water to penetrate to the soil below and can expand and contract without cracking. In addition, because the color of the granite is lighter and its density is much lower than either concrete or asphalt, it captures and retains less heat from the sun. Other walkway paving consists of precast concrete step-stones surrounded by stabilized granite to create a smooth path that allows water to penetrate. If necessary, these step-stones can be easily relocated or replaced, preserving the energy that would be necessary to replace concrete walkways.

A small area in the entryway of the home consists of a special brick pavement manufactured on the East Coast. The brick is made partially from soil removed from areas surrounding old gasoline tanks and other oil-laden land. The manufacturer fires the polluted material in a high-temperature kiln, burning off any oil residue and creating a strong paving brick suitable for construction. Three problems prevented a more extensive use of this material as paving throughout the exterior areas of the home. First, shipping the bricks from the East Coast to Phoenix was expensive. Second, there was no reliable data showing that the oil toxins would not leach out into the soil over time. Third, because the brick would have been used in several heavy load situations, as in front of the garage, in the house, and by the pool, it would have been necessary to pour a concrete slab first, which would not have been resource efficient.

Sitework

Termites, though not a major problem in the Southwestern desert, do occasionally invade a home, making termite prevention an important consideration for Valley homebuilders. Jones Studio investigated several nonchemical termite treatments for the ESH. One nonchemical treatment consists of a termite barrier made of specialized sand installed under the slabs of the home. The material is made up of the sand particles that fall between a ten-mesh screen and a sixteen-mesh screen: the resulting configuration includes small particles that are too tightly packed for termites to tunnel through and larger ones that are too large for their mandibles to pick up. Unfortunately, the specially sized sand costs nearly $90 per ton delivered from California, compared to $9 per ton for standard masonry sand available locally. Though the barrier probably would have been effective much longer than would any chemical treatment, it was not available for delivery to the ESH in time for installation or at a reasonable cost. Therefore, the architects chose a water-based permethrin chemical treatment for this area.

Permethrin, one of three kinds of synthetic pyrethroid, is an analog of the botanical insecticide pyrethrum, a chemical occurring naturally in many flowers. Its main advantage over other insecticides is its photodegradability: if it is spilled or applied excessively above ground, sunlight will degrade it into harmless components in thirty to sixty days, while petroleum-based alternatives may remain toxic for years.

**Pouring of flyash-
reinforced concrete**

The water-based permethrin also affects air quality much less during the application process than do solvent-based termiticides. Though treatments derived from pyrethroid are effective for five to seven years compared with the ten to twenty years of petroleum derivatives, during that time they are more effective at stopping termites.

One last item in the sitework was the radon-mitigation system. Radon is an odorless, radioactive gas formed in the earth during the decomposition or decay of radioactive elements such as radium and uranium. Radon, if present, can seep into buildings through cracks in foundations. Although radon is not a common problem in Arizona, high concentrations of radon have been identified in scattered sites in the metropolitan area, and the costs for cleanup after construction can be enormous.

Before the home was cleared for foundation work, Radiation Safety Engineering carried out special testing at 50-foot intervals on the lot to determine the levels of radon (RA-226) in the soil. Although findings indicated that radon poses no problem at this site, the EPA asked that the following system (DOC.EPA/625/2-91/032) be installed as

a demonstration of a simple and inexpensive method of reducing radon exposure. The Radon Passive Sub-Slab Depressurization System consists of a 4-inch-diameter, perforated PVC pipe running down the center length of the home in the gravel below the slab. This pipe vents through a vertical pipe that emerges through the roof at a location at least 10 feet from the nearest window or door. In addition to natural ventilation, the system uses the discrepancy between the air pressure under the home and the air outside the home to draw radon gas out before it can seep through the floor slab. Should this airflow system not be enough, a small fan can be added to the vent pipe at a later date and run periodically to expel a greater amount of air.

Foundations/Slabs

The desert's climate, with its extremes of temperature, pushes and pulls materials in an expansion and contraction cycle until they crack and finally fail. One of the most durable materials to use in the desert is concrete because its stonelike properties allow it to fend off the climatic changes. In addition, it is essentially chemically inert and will eventually erode into materials similar to stone and gravel. However, concrete is not entirely an environmentally efficient material because its primary ingredient, portland cement, is produced by the calcination of lime dust. The calcination process is very energy intensive, resulting in the high embodied energy characteristic of concrete.

The use of concrete in construction is inevitable, because it can be easily formed into high-strength shapes for footings and floor slabs. Because it holds up so well in the desert, its use here is even more prevalent than in other areas of the country, showing up not only in foundations and floor slabs, but also in columns, beams, and even walls. To make the use of concrete in the ESH energy efficient, the architects sought an alternative method of manufacture that would reduce the embodied energy of the product while also reinforcing it with recycled materials.

Though portland cement is the primary ingredient in concrete, a portion of it can be replaced in most applied situations with "flyash." By coincidence, flyash is a byproduct of coal-fired electricity production, as done at APS's Cholla Power Plant in northeastern Arizona.

Pollution scrubbers collect flyash in the power plant smokestacks, which prevent air-polluting emissions from escaping to the atmosphere. It is then cleaned out of the scrubbers and removed to landfills. However, when mixed with water, flyash has cementlike properties and can easily replace 30 percent of the cement in concrete. In the ESH, flyash collected from the Cholla Power Plant replaces 25 percent of the cement in the foundation and slab concrete, significantly reducing the embodied energy of the concrete and reducing the amount of flyash sent to landfills. Flyash makes the concrete mix pour and trowel more easily. It also strengthens the concrete, perhaps as much as 10 to 15 percent; therefore, less concrete is required, resulting in even greater savings.

Steel rods often reinforce concrete areas. The architects specified recycled metal for all reinforcing steel in the home. The metal used is industrial steel with a high recycled content, primarily from discarded automobiles. This recycled product has been long available for home construction. Steel reinforcement rods, metal studs, and the metal roof of the ESH have all been manufactured with this high-recycled-content metal.

Though concrete has a high-energy content, there are ways to make it save energy in other areas, such as in floor applications where so much material is required. Residential construction in the Southwest typically uses what is called the "slab-on-grade" technique. This technique involves a carefully prepared and leveled subgrade over which is poured a concrete slab that becomes the structural floor for the house. Over this concrete slab, already full of embodied energy, are laid more energy-intensive products such as carpet, vinyl tile, and other floor coverings. This concrete slab, with little extra effort, can be the finished floor instead. In the ESH, the architects added color to the concrete and created a variety of finishes for different areas of the home, from a sandy, stone-like texture to a highly polished, smooth surface. It was necessary to use some ceramic tile and carpet in the home, but these materials were placed only where they were needed to limit water penetration in bathrooms or to warm bedroom floors. Even these limited-use materials were carefully selected: as we see later in this chapter, the carpeting and the floor tiles are made of unusual recycled materials.

Troweling concrete for outdoor living area

Insulation is added to exterior walls
Background: concrete masonry units in place

Expansion joints are necessary wherever large areas of concrete come in contact with each other or with fixed objects such as stem walls or columns. The joints require a compressible filler that allows the concrete to move just enough so that it does not bind and crack, an important consideration in the ESH where so much of the floor slab is exposed as the finished material. For the home, a 100-percent-recycled newsprint product was chosen to fill in the expansion joints, not only protecting the entire perimeter of the home, but also creating an aesthetic pattern on the floor in the interior, where "control joints" were cut into the slab inside the home for expansion.

Envelope Walls/Insulation

Out of several possible alternatives, the architects decided to use a locally produced concrete block, Integra Block, to form the exterior envelope, or outside walls, of the home. The criteria for choice were that the system be structurally sound, be properly insulated, provide an aesthetic interior and exterior finish, and make use of materials as resource-efficient as possible. One possible alternative, a form created of foam

block into which concrete is poured to make a structural wall, raised concerns about the amount of extra exterior and interior finish materials that would be needed and the amount of concrete and reinforcing materials that would be required in construction. A second alternative, wood-frame construction and stucco, is used for much production housing, even here in the desert, miles from any forest. As wood is becoming more and more expensive due to its growing scarcity, its use for framing the ESH would not have been the most resource-efficient choice. A third alternative, standard concrete masonry units (CMUs), or concrete block, met the criterion of structural soundness, but did not meet the criterion of insulation or aesthetic interior or exterior finish.

The product that best met all the criteria was the 8-inch-thick Integra Block CMU. Locally manufactured by the Superlite Block Company of Phoenix, the Integra Block used for the ESH consists of 25 percent flyash, a byproduct of APS's coal-fired plants. The block is a simple H shape, filled with insulation. It has only one thermal bridge point between the faces of the block; the thermal bridge point is the weak link in the insulative qualities of any concrete block where heat is allowed to go around the insulation and pass through the wall. The architects' goal was to surpass the standard R-19 value available with the typical 6-inch stud-framed wall usually filled with fiberglass insulation. To meet this goal, they used not only the small thermal bridge point of the Integra Block, but also an effective insulation material to fill the hollow spaces of the block. The insulation chosen has a value of R-24, providing about 25 percent more insulation than that of standard materials.

Integra Block is currently used in a few production home developments in the Valley, but all use Integra's standard polyurethane foam for insulation. As explained in chapter 2, substituting Supergreen Foam for the standard foam results in a wall system that is both energy efficient and environmentally responsible. The combination of block and foam has an added benefit over frame-wall construction; the mass of the block and the vibration resistance of the foam stops sound waves, resulting in a sound rating two times higher than that of wood-frame stucco. With the house situated next to busy Greenway Road, the

future owners will appreciate the noise reduction of the block and foam.

Typical finishes of CMUs are either paint and/or stucco for exteriors and gypsum wallboard and paint for interiors, adding to the embodied energy of the walls and the cost of the construction, but not improving the resistance to weather of the block itself. In fact, these finishes add to the lifetime maintenance cost of the system because of the need to repaint or to repair the stucco. To avoid painting the Integra Blocks, the architects decided to have the surface sandblasted so that the thin gray outer layer was removed to expose the colorful, textured aggregate inside, thus achieving a finish for the block without added materials and the cost of stuccoing and painting. A penetrating sealer provides lifetime water protection, making the wall essentially maintenance free. This feature of Integra Block is its major advantage over other wall systems: the stucco and other finish materials required by most wall systems represent an increase in materials used and resources wasted.

A final feature of the Integra Block exterior wall system is Integra's "post-tensioning" system in which tension

rods are brought up through the wall and secured by special cap blocks about every 4 feet of wall length. This process reinforces the masonry, eliminating much of the grout typically needed in concrete block walls. It also reduces the amount of manufactured material that must be added to the wall, while increasing the amount of space available for the Supergreen insulation material, improving the wall's overall insulation value.

There were some sections of the exterior walls, however, that needed to be constructed of framing materials made of wood or wood products. These sections included areas where large amounts of plumbing or electrical systems were to be placed, odd-shaped areas such as the triangular gable ends of the home where the block would have to be cut to fit, or nonstructural areas where block would be unnecessary. In these areas, the architects chose to use an engineered wood product known as finger-jointed lumber for the framing of the home. Finger-jointing is a process by which timber is sawn and then processed to remove the knots and other low-quality areas of the wood. The resulting lengths of lumber, some as

Engineered lumber

Uses small-diameter, fast-growing trees

Allows more of the tree to be used

Has greater strength and stiffness

Can accommodate longer spans

Can be prefabricated to exact lengths, thus preventing waste

Dimensional lumber

Subject to shortages and rising costs

Uses wood from old-growth forests

Has tendency to warp and crack

15. Engineered lumber vs. solid-sawn dimensional lumber

short as 18 inches, are then run through a special saw that cuts a series of small "teeth" in the wood and allows the pieces to be fit together, joined with glue, and planed to match the size of standard dimensional lumber. The resulting product is straighter, stronger, and more stable than a solid piece of lumber. It is also more resistant to warping and cracking than are standard wood studs, making construction simpler, faster, and less wasteful.

Finger-jointed wood studs (2 inches by 6 inches) are an example of engineered wood, a class of products made of particles and small pieces that would otherwise go to waste in the production process (table 15). Another product made of engineered wood used in the ESH is oriented strand board (OSB), a commonly used but very resource-efficient material used to sheath the exterior wood walls and roof of both the home and the garage. This material was first developed in the late 1970s in response to a limited availability of wood and a large increase in its price. Because the price increase made plywood too expensive to use in many nonstructural areas of homes, several companies searched for alternative ways

to make wood sheet material. The result was OSB, or "waferboard," as it was first known. It is composed of panels of strandlike particles, which are arranged in layers oriented at right angles to one another. Three to five layers are bound with adhesive and then compressed and sanded to produce a rigid sheet product. In the early years of its production, the manufacturing processes and adhesive choices were not well developed, so delaminating and shearing were problems. Initially OSB was not structurally rated, so its use was confined to backing material and other redundant locations. Since then, it has been much improved and has been approved for most structural applications, including roof, wall, and floor locations, even where shear capability is necessary. The architects originally planned to use OSB for only the main house roof sheathing, but they found that its cost competitiveness made it feasible to use in all sheathing applications.

OSB has many resource-efficient characteristics. Because it is made from flakes of wood, almost the entire tree can be used. The flakes can be carefully selected to eliminate low-grade wood and knot areas, so that the finished product is stronger. It can also be manufactured in varying sizes that permit better use of the panels at the job site, eliminating construction waste. Most importantly, though, OSB uses low-grade, young, fast-growing trees of different species from those commonly used for plywood, thus displacing the use of large plywood-grade "peeler logs" typically harvested from old-growth timber.

Exterior wood frame walls present another energy-related problem—they often allow air to infiltrate the structure. To counteract this, the architects specified several barriers to air movement. One type of barrier, the frame wall sill plate (where the frame wall connects to the block wall or the floor slab) is sealed against air infiltration by using a "sill sealer," a foam strip placed under the sill plate and compressed as the sill plate is fastened down, filling the gaps between the floor slab and the wood frame wall. Made of recycled materials, the sill sealer contains a minimum of 50 percent postconsumer recovered polystyrene. On the outside of the wall sheathing, an air infiltration barrier, consisting of a thin but durable woven plastic sheet, stretches over the sheathing to cover all the gaps and to prevent air from leaking into or out of the house.

Nature Guard cellulose insulation fills the wood-frame walls and ceiling, forming a tight, even seal around wiring, plumbing, and framing materials. Insulation makes up a large percentage of the amount of construction materials and hence the embodied energy of the home. Insulation material must not only make the home more energy efficient, but be produced in an energy-efficient manner. The standard choice of insulation is usually fiberglass, but fiberglass requires a large amount of energy in its production, even when it incorporates recycled glass. Nature Guard, made entirely of compressed recycled newspapers, requires only a fraction of the energy to produce as compared to fiberglass. To make it fire resistant, a fire-retarding chemical is mixed with the paper. Nature Guard is also energy efficient, with an R-value of 3.8 per inch and is much more efficient than batts at filling voids. Overall, the Nature Guard-filled fingerjointed stud walls provide an R-value of at least 22.

This nontoxic insulation does not contain formaldehyde, asbestos, or fiberglass. According to *Environmental*

Insulation made of recycled newspapers is blown into walls *Background:* **detail of insulation**

Concrete block, Trex siding, and TJI joists

Building News, environmental concerns about cellulose dust, inks, and fire-retarding additives of Nature Guard have recently been shown to be unfounded. The newspaper industry has taken steps to eliminate toxins from its products. Another benefit of this material, which will probably grow in popularity in the building industry, is that installation does not expose workers to irritating fiberglass particulates.

Because the ESH is a showcase home designed to demonstrate more than one product for some applications, and because a second resource-efficient type of insulation was available, it was used in the garage roof. Air krete is a cementitious foam product made from dehydrated sea water and refractory cement, an inert byproduct of several industrial chemical processes. This product contains no petroleum, CFCs, or volatile organic compounds (VOCs). A fireproof, nontoxic product, air krete has an insulative R-value of 3.9 per inch. Because it is an expanding foam it fills voids that even blown cellulose cannot.

The only major drawback is its high cost, because the production is a proprietary process and the product currently is available from only one installer in the

Phoenix area. It requires minimal production energy, can be economically transported as a liquid, is blown into walls with CO_2 (the gas we exhale and plants breathe) and, much like cellulose, is very effective at sound deadening. It is also a good retrofit material and can be added to existing walls to increase their insulative values.

To complete the few exterior frame walls not made of natural concrete block, it was necessary to choose stucco and siding for the finish. The stucco used is an integrally colored, three-coat cementitious stucco with flyash added. The stucco's integral color should never need painting, while the flyash adds embodied energy reduction benefits.

The Trex composite lumber used for the siding is a very sophisticated combination of recycled plastic and wood fiber, each lending its traits to make an advanced type of "plastic lumber." Trex is a mixture of recycled high-density polyethylene (HDPE), made primarily of plastic grocery bags, milk jugs, and wood fiber, some of which is recycled pallet wood. The plastic acts as the binder and preservative for the wood, while the wood adds slip resistance and dimensional stability, both lacking in other lumber substitutes that are made of all plastic. The result is a product that can withstand moisture, heat, and dryness better than wood does and can be installed without concern about expansion/contraction or sagging in outdoor environments as with other plastic products. Though it is commonly used for outdoor decks and railings, the architects chose to use it as a siding (perhaps the first such use of this product), because there is much interest in an alternative to stucco for exterior walls of structures in the desert. Natural wood fails in just a few years even when rigorously maintained; metal siding has found little acceptance; and though fiber-cement products endure, they are as expensive, if not more so, than the composite lumber and have much lower recycled content than Trex. In addition, all of these alternatives require a finish of some sort. An added benefit of Trex is that though it can be sealed or painted, it does not need to be—it can weather over time to a soft gray color like aged cedar.

Roof Framing

The ESH's roof is framed with a variety of resource-efficient wood products

from an innovative company called Trus Joist MacMillan. Although recycled steel has some advantages over wood framing, Jones Studio chose wood over steel for several reasons, most notably its insulative qualities. Because the home is designed with a vaulted ceiling without an attic and the roof framing becomes part of the thermal envelope of the home, wood insulates the home far better than steel does. Wood is and will likely continue to be a primary material in residential construction, and the design of this home provides the opportunity to exhibit the latest technology in wood framing. Though some of these materials are already used in production homebuilding in the Phoenix area, this is one of the first projects to combine so many of the products in one home.

Trus Joist MacMillan manufactures four materials used in this home. All adhesives and binders used in their products are composed of phenol formaldehyde, which does not continue to off-gas after manufacture and has little effect on indoor air quality. There is a single continuous Parallam ridge beam, with TJI or Microllam joists spanning up to it from the outside walls, and Timber-Strand lumber used for the subfascia

TJI Joist/Parallam connection

Embodied Energy Costs of Building Materials

Reuse represents the best and highest level of resource efficiency for the home. If one considers the extraction, refinement, and manufacturing processes alone, the relative energy intensity of various building materials can be represented by the following list (the lower the number, the less energy is required to produce the product).

lumber = 1
cement = 2
glass = 3
fiberglass = 7
steel = 8
plastic = 30
aluminum = 80

(From the *Design Issues Guide*, created for APS by EcoGroup, Inc. and the Center for Resourceful Building Technology) and the header above the clerestory. The only solid-sawn lumber used is for the two-by-four horizontal framing of the clerestory roof pitch.

Parallam, known generically as parallel strand lumber (PSL), is a heavy timber beam made from strands of wood 1-inch wide, 1/8-inch thick, and 8-feet long, produced by peeling small-diameter, fast-growing trees. The peeled veneers are chopped to a width of 1 inch, and all low-grade wood and knots are cut out. The strips are then combined with adhesive, compressed, microwave-dried, and sawn to dimensional lumber sizes up to 7 1/2-inches wide, 18-inches deep, and 66-feet long. The Parallam process can use nearly all the wood in a tree. Its nearest competitor, the "gluelam" beam, is made by gluing together much larger dimensional lumber, which requires the harvesting of larger, older trees.

The I-joists used in the structural roof framing of the home are also made from engineered wood rather than from traditional solid-sawn lumber. Using a combination of Microllam flanges (described below) and an oriented strand board web, the manufacturer was able to design a structurally efficient I-shaped

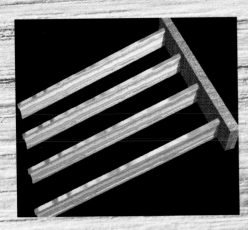

Roof structure
Background: detail of
Parallam PSL

joist that puts the bulk of the wood on the top and bottom of the I-shape, where the greatest amount of structural strength is needed.

Microllam, known generically as laminated veneer lumber (LVL), looks much like very thick plywood cut into lengths and stood on edge. The plys in Microllam are a bit thicker than those in plywood, but essentially the production is the same. Trees are peeled, making large sheets that are then graded, with the lesser peels going to the Parallam production line because defects can be more selectively cut out. In this way, nearly all the structural grade wood of the tree is used. The high-grade peels remaining after grading are laid up in very large mats with an adhesive, then compressed, dried, sanded, and cut to precise sizes, up to 1 3/4-inches thick, 14-inches deep, and 66-feet long. Microllam boards have very good bending strength and shear capability, so they work well as an intermediary in strength between the TJIs and Parallams for short, light load headers or joists with point loads.

TimberStrand is perhaps the most innovative of these products because it makes use of the aspen, an otherwise

nonstructural-grade tree, as its source. The aspen tree is very common in the northern part of the United States. Though it grows rapidly, it has found little use in construction because of its poor natural strength, small diameter, knotty character, and poor straightness. The tree has a short life span and usually lives less than a century, as compared with the several-century life span of a structural grade fir or pine. Trus Joist MacMillan has pioneered a way to make use of this fast-growing resource. In a manner similar to OSB production, aspen trees are chipped into flakes, which are then graded to eliminate low-grade wood and knots. The flakes are combined with adhesive into huge mats, which are compressed, dried, sanded, and cut. The result is a laminated strand lumber (LSL) that is actually stronger than solid-sawn lumber and can be used for longer spans. Continued use of non-traditional woods such as aspen may eventually take the burden off of slow-growing old-growth forests.

Roof

The RTS Standing Seam Shingles roofing material, made of 60 percent recycled steel, is a good example of a single product that achieves several environmental goals. Its recycled content means that fewer waste materials are ending up in a landfill. Its light weight is another important benefit—half as much as an asphalt shingle and as little as 15 percent of the weight of a concrete or clay tile roof. This translates into a savings in the materials needed for structural support such as walls, columns, and even foundations. There is a high total savings in embodied energy because of the light weight of the roof.

In addition to its recycled content and its weight, another environmental benefit of the roofing material is that the metal reflects sunlight, lowering cooling costs in the summer. The lighter mass of the roof also results in less retained heat and faster shedding after sunset of the heat gained during the day, thus saving cooling energy for the home. For the homeowner, advantages include the durability and fire protection of metal roofing. The roofing system demonstrates how materials for homebuilding can have multiple impacts on natural resources. This one product saves energy in many different ways.

In flat roof areas, such as in the entry, the roof is finished with a product known as Mirrorseal, a membrane roofing that is applied as a liquid. The base of the product, made of saltwater, is completely nontoxic and contains no hazardous materials.

The environmental advantage of Mirrorseal is obvious when compared to petroleum-based roofing systems such as tar roofs and gravel-coat asphalt. It is fire resistant, easy to apply, and acts as both an insulator and reflector, protecting the interior of the entry. Its white color reflects 82 percent of the sun's rays, so its use over confined spaces would result in energy savings through heat load reduction.

Interior Wall Framing

The interior of the home is framed with American Studco metal studs that contain up to 60 percent recycled steel. Steel studs are leftovers, or "cut-offs," from the construction process that can be reused, and the entire item can be recycled after demolition or remodeling. Using steel studs offsets the use of dwindling supplies of solid-sawn wood lumber typically used in this application and can result in straighter walls because the steel does not warp or twist like wood.

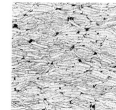

Details of building materials

Steel studs in interior walls

The wall finishes are gypsum wallboard, Nailer drywall stop, and paint. Gypsum wallboard (or drywall) is economical and has 100 percent recycled paper face sheets. Gypsum wallboard is recyclable in many large cities and can be made from waste gypsum generated from several manufacturing processes. The Nailer drywall stop is made from recycled plastic and eliminates the need for up to two studs at corners and a ledger at the top of walls. This saves material and labor while eliminating thermal bridges and allowing for more insulation in the wall where the studs were eliminated.

Interior

The choice of finishings for the home's interior was driven by the important consideration of indoor air quality. Unhealthy indoor air quality is typical of the problems arising from modern technological advances. Since the oil shortages of the 1970s, architects and builders have made concerted efforts to use energy more efficiently, resulting in changes in the way they build, insulate, heat, cool, and ventilate homes. Consequently, buildings have become more heavily insulated, and, although they conserve energy, "tight buildings" can also trap and maintain indoor air pollutants, resulting in what is known as the "sick building syndrome," which includes symptoms such as irritation of the eyes, nose, and throat; dry sensations in the mucous and skin; erythema; mental fatigue; and the perception of weak but persistent odors.

The indoor environment may contain air contaminated by a variety of sources: off-gasses from building materials, infiltration from contaminants outside the building, and indoor activities. There are three approaches to reducing indoor air pollution: source control (the most cost-effective), ventilation (improper ventilation accounts for over half of the complaints about indoor air quality), and air cleaning/filtering (which is most effective when combined with one or both of the other two methods).

For source control, the architects used a minimum of paints, varnishes, and sealers and chose natural surfaces and fibers wherever possible. Where paints and sealers were necessary, environmentally responsible alternatives were found. Traditional carpet adhesives, a major culprit in unhealthy indoor air because of their alcohol, glycol, or ammonia content, were replaced by Envirotec Healthguard Adhesive, a product that is antimicrobial, contains no carcinogenic materials, and does not emit any hazardous vapors. The carpet pad, made from 100 percent recycled jute fiber, has few off-gassing problems because of its natural fiber content.

Because of the unique concrete flooring described earlier, the use of carpeting in the home is kept to a minimum. The design of the carpeting layout further reduces the amount used: in the bedrooms, circles are removed from the wall-to-wall carpet at the foot of the bed and are used as rugs in strategic areas in the living room and dining room. Also, the rooms are sized so that a standard roll of carpet will fit without the need for cutting and trimming, thus eliminating waste. The carpet itself is made of 100 percent recycled polyethylene (PET) from soft drink and ketchup bottles. Not only does this material save plastic bottles from the landfills, it also reduces the use of imported crude oil, the standard raw material for carpet.

Jones Studio also chose to finish the interior surfaces of the home with materials that do not contribute to indoor air pollution. The three wall coverings used,

Medite fiberboard, Homasote burlap panels, and sanded OSB, have different features that make them environmentally friendly. The fiberboard, used for the cabinetry substructure, interior wallboard, portions of the paneling, interior door frames, and selected interior trim, uses wood sawdust particles bonded together with a formaldehyde-free binder. It produces a very resource-efficient, high-strength material whose durability translates into extended longevity, thus saving resources for its replacement. The burlap panels, used as interior accent wallboard or paneling near some of the desks and office work areas, are constructed of 100 percent recycled newsprint covered with a natural jute fabric. The fabric conceals pin or tack holes, while the unit provides extra thermal insulation and sound deadening. The OSB, used elsewhere on the home as the sheathing on the exterior walls and roof, has been sanded and given a clear seal finish that enhances its wood grain design for a distinctive interior accent.

Drawer fronts in some of the cabinets of the dining room are crafted of a fiberboard that is made from recycled paper and other products bound together by

Interior surfaces were chosen for minimum off-gassing potential

**Bedroom shows use of
natural materials and
fibers for furnishings**

water and soy flour. This resin and cellulose mixture cures without releasing any
toxins into the air.

Source control is the most effective
method of controlling indoor air pollution, but the ESH also demonstrates
several products available for ventilation
and air cleaning, including high-quality
filters, air exchangers, and a central vacuum system. When the motorized
clerestory windows are open, natural
ventilation circulates fresh air throughout the home. For those months that
heating and air conditioning are not
needed, the house fan draws air in from
outside and distributes it through the
home through the duct system. The
central vacuum system solves a major
problem of indoor cleaning of carpets
and furniture. With traditional vacuum
cleaners, many of the microscopic contaminants that the cleaner picks up are
actually released back into the house.
The ESH's built-in system, on the other
hand, exhausts the air to the outside,
thus avoiding recirculating any contaminants into the interior air of the home.

The furnishings for the home were
chosen by the designers at Allegro
Business Interiors. Their research into
environmentally friendly furnishings led

them to several innovative companies around the world, and one well-known company in Arizona, that design and build furniture on principles of sustainability. From Germany, Willkhahn, Inc., is a company that bases all of its activities and products on an ecological foundation. From Montana, the Green Toy Store supplied toys made of postconsumer recycled materials. The designers felt that children would benefit from learning the importance of closing the recycling loop. In the children's bedroom is the Geoseat, made partly of recycled postconsumer HDPE plastic that has been compression molded and partly of HDPE that has been extruded. This is a unique use of two different types of recycling processes. Finally, from Arizona, a new company known as Natural Cotton Colours, Inc., has developed cotton plants that produce colored fibers that can be woven into fabric that needs no bleaching or dyeing. The company's FoxFibre cotton is used on several of the home's furnishings.

Other interior features demonstrate the versatility of recycled materials. The tile in the bathrooms is an unglazed ceramic tile made of post-industrial recycled auto windshield glass. In the kitchen, the floor tile is made from twice-recycled marble chips and dust left over from the manufacture of marble tiles. Part of the kitchen countertop area is actually made from postindustrial recycled plastic made to look like granite. In the guest bath, the vanity top is made from 90 percent recycled HDPE such as milk jugs, plastic containers, and plastic bags. All these uses of recycled materials help to create a market for the goods we throw away, thus keeping them out of landfills and preserving the raw materials that would be necessary to generate new products.

Construction Waste

Reduction of construction debris, which constitutes a large portion of the material destined for landfills, is one of the most frequently overlooked areas for resource conservation. According to Steve Loken of the Center for Resourceful Building Technology, the building of a typical single-family home produces an average of four to six tons of waste per building site. It is anticipated that 18,000 new homes will be built annually in the Phoenix area in the 1990s, a rate

Construction waste recycling containers, with detail above

Material	Lbs.	Percent of total	Embodied energy (BTU's)
Lumber	1,250	25	3,954,297
Sheetrock	750	15	2,492,857
Plywood	500	10	2,570,000
Bricks/Masonry	600	12	2,245,715
Cardboard	500	10	—
Asphalt	300	6	—
Fiberglass	250	5	2,450,000
Metals	200	4	—
Plastics	200	4	—
Other	950	9	—
Total	5,500	100	13,712,869

16. Estimated embodied energy in construction debris for a new 2,500-square-foot home

Source: Adapted from AIA (1993)

that could generate over 100,000 tons of construction waste yearly. Construction waste is often considered clean because it lacks the hazardous elements commonly found in household waste, although a possibility exists that the paints, sealers, and caulking found in this waste stream could contribute to groundwater contamination.

Because construction waste contains valuable secondary resources, it makes good sense to conserve and recycle left-over building materials. Chris Rossi, in a recent article in *Recycling Review* on how builders can cut down on building waste, had the following to say about decreasing construction waste:

The nature of the residential construction waste stream provides many opportunities for builders to begin looking for alternative means of disposal, such as contracting with local waste haulers and recyclers to set up jobsite bins for wood, metals, wallboard, cardboard, and other recyclable items. The extra effort to separate materials at the site can be compensated for by lowering tipping fees at the landfill. Some commercial waste haulers have dedicated their operations to handling of C&D [construction and demolition] waste.

A successful California waste hauler uses a three-phase C&D operation that matches the production schedule of a house. In the first phase, the recycler dumpster receives wood and metal scraps from the framing of the house. The second stage assigns foam and drywall, followed by a stage for cardboard from appliance boxes and scrap wood from finishing.

Choosing a material that is durable, non-flammable, and represents an efficient use of resources also can greatly reduce the amount of waste left over from building operations. . . . Builders can also specify the use of engineered wood products designed to reduce the estimated 70 percent of dimensional lumber content of the wood in their waste piles.

APS, together with Browning-Ferris Industries, a waste-disposal company, and Homes & Son, the general contractor, established a waste-management reuse program at the ESH jobsite based on the following elements:

1. Separation of construction waste material into separate bins at the site
2. Purchase of material in required dimensions to minimize waste
3. Reuse of as many discarded materials as possible in the building process
4. Reuse of material from sources other than the ESH.

A good example of this last management element was the use of old, discarded carpeting material to protect the concrete floors while construction on the ESH continued. On its way to a local landfill, the used carpet was "discovered" and diverted to the ESH, where it was used one more time before disposal.

There were several problems with the construction-site recycling bins. One was that the process for pickup and delivery of the bins was cumbersome. In addition, the bins took up a large amount of space on the site. A third problem, discovered after the home was completed, was that a larger amount of waste went to the landfill than had been expected.

A possible reason for this last problem is that, because this is a showcase home with several different systems displayed for individual house functions, there was simply more waste from the array of different materials. These problems will have to be solved in the future so that this valuable process of reusing and recycling construction waste can be implemented more easily.

Reusing material from homebuilding benefits the environment because the embodied energy of the reused materials is salvaged and then reused. In 1993, the *Environmental Resource Guide* of the American Institute of Architects (AIA) estimated the amount of embodied energy in the construction debris from one typical new home. Table 16 is adapted from the AIA analysis; the breakdown of construction debris from a 2,500-square-foot house is shown by the type of material, its weight, and its estimated embodied energy in BTUs. If this waste material can be diverted and reused, then one of the goals of sustainable development, resource efficiency, is closer to being achieved.

Backyard Composting Demonstration

A composting system has been installed at the ESH for demonstration purposes. Considered an important environmental trend of the 1990s, composting is a natural biological process in

Steps in a life cycle assessment

1. Identify raw material and associated costs for harvesting that material for use

2. Identify all energy, materials, and chemicals used as input to the manufacturing process and hazards associated with their use

3. Identify all materials and chemicals generated in the manufacturing process and hazards associated with their production

4. Identify disposal methods for waste products and impacts to air, water, and other environmental concerns

5. Identify materials used in packaging the product for shipment

6. Identify energy used in transporting of the product to its final destination

7. Identify resources used during the use of the product, such as energy consumption

8. Identify the method of disposal for the product, whether it can be recycled or must go to a landfill

17. The life cycle assessment process

Source: Curran (1994)

which organic materials from plants or animals are decomposed under controlled conditions to produce a stable humus material useful as a soil amendment or mulch. Many organic materials can be used to form compost, but the most common materials for residential backyard compost piles are yard and landscaping waste (grass clippings, leaves, branches, wood), food waste (except meat and dairy products), paper, and cardboard.

Composting is considered an important factor in closing the recycling loop because it can transform an otherwise unrecyclable but significant portion of the waste stream into a useful product. In addition to conserving valuable landfill space, composting is relatively easy, requiring only a shovel to occasionally turn the pile. It is also safe because it is a natural process and no chemicals are required, and it may actually improve lawn and garden quality. The decomposition process releases valuable nutrients and moisture to the soil, decreasing the need for artificial fertilizers; it helps to suppress plant disease without the use of toxic pesticides; and it encourages bigger root systems for healthier plants.

Shortcomings in the Selection Process

The materials selection process was set up to choose the best available resource-efficient material for each use within the home. One problem was that, despite careful and time-consuming decision making, no systematic decision criteria were applied to the process that would allow for an objective comparative appraisal of the available materials to show degrees of difference between one material and another. A procedure known as the Life Cycle Assessment (LCA), one of the few methods available today to accomplish such a comparative appraisal, was used to test some of the materials, but not all.

LCA is based on a "cradle-to-grave" approach, where all inputs and outputs that are used or produced in the manufacturing of a product are accounted for (table 17). This includes resource depletion, energy use, air and water pollution, and solid waste generation. To be effective, this analysis begins when the raw materials are extracted from the ground and continues through the disposal of the product after its useful life. LCA allows a homebuilder to identify the environmental burdens and social costs that are associated with selected home construction materials.

Once these burdens are recognized, processes can be redesigned to decrease the amount or types of resources used. Even packaging can be changed. LCA is a tool that can assist in making the right choices of materials by considering such factors as which manufacturing process produces the least amount of harmful byproducts, which products use fewer natural resources, and how recycling or disposal of the product is handled. An LCA, carried out at the beginning of the selection process, could have provided the design team with an objective comparative valuation of the materials of the home. A problem with the LCA method, however, is that it is a science that is not fully developed as yet, and it may not have been practical for the large number of materials needed in this home.

In spite of these problems, it would have been beneficial to employ the LCA at the beginning of the materials selection process: instead, it was used to evaluate three systems of the home after the selection process was over. Science Certification Systems (SCS) of Oakland, California, was hired to verify the claims of the manufacturers and also to do a "first-order" estimate of the environmental benefits of three of the home's systems—the roof, the walls, and the floors. A preliminary analysis of the data shows that, for the materials used in the three major elements of the home, there are generally discernable environmental benefits when compared to materials used in conventional homes. The data also suggest that the long-term energy savings due to materials selected will be significant.

Another problem with the results of the materials selection process is almost the mirror image of the first. If APS had made the decision consciously *not* to use a scientific method to choose the "best" material, then its obligation to the public was to showcase a wider selection of available materials.

This would have allowed the home buyer and homebuilder to visit a true "shopping center" of construction ideas. Instead, the public is limited to a "boutique" where all the selections have already been made. Admittedly, a number of items were not selected because of prohibitive costs or availability problems.

Regional Sustainability

In an era when the number and size of homes being built in the United States are steadily rising, projects like the APS Environmental Showcase Home are valuable. They demonstrate to the homebuilding industry and to home buyers that a structure can be much less intensive in its use of resources than that of a typical new home, yet still be a quality product. People need to know that a home can be both resource efficient and energy efficient without compromising the other values that the market demands.

The ESH also illustrates the use of bioregionally appropriate materials to help buyers understand that the design and materials most suited to Arizona's extreme climate are probably not the same ones best suited to Seattle's climate. Locally produced materials and regionally adapted designs are important components of environmentally responsible building. Projects like the ESH remind people to build in a manner appropriate for their location and climate.

Showing homebuilders recycled-content building materials installed in an exemplary structure like the ESH encourages them to learn about these materials and use them in their own projects. This project makes important new technology more accessible to everyone involved in building construction. As both buyers and builders learn to use resource-efficient materials, the incredible natural resource demand caused by residential building can be dramatically lessened.

Steve Loken
Center for Resourceful Building Technology

In spite of the above-mentioned shortcomings in the process, a surprisingly wide array of materials is showcased. What the method lacked in scientific rigor, it made up for in sheer devotion to comprehensiveness by the APS project team and the architects of Jones Studio.

The Significance of Materials

In spite of the problems mentioned with materials selection, the ESH has demonstrated that it is indeed possible to do more with less. It is possible to take the things we throw away, such as glass bottles, newspapers, and old automobiles, and transform them into energy- and resource-efficient home construction materials. It is possible to create materials that do not poison our indoor air. It is possible to find materials that were manufactured using a minimum-impact process. All of these possibilities have become part of a large store of knowledge that can be used again and again in the Valley, if the public and the homebuilders of the area become aware of the concepts explored by the ESH.

Superficially, building materials are the most easily understood of environmentally conscious building practices. The public knows that "recycled" means "good." What is harder to understand is the complex nature of a cradle-to-grave process of a given material. One has to answer such questions as: What is the source material of the product? What was the nature of the manufacturing process it went through? Is it recyclable itself? Is it durable? What is its total embodied energy content? Is it safe? Add to this such considerations as cost, availability, code compliance, and aesthetics, and we can see the difficult nature of the decision-making process. As the public learns more about these and other materials that minimize our impact on the environment, the benefits of the difficult decision-making process undertaken by APS and Jones Studio and their consultants are available to anyone who is ready to build a home, or a subdivision of homes, that is truly environmentally friendly.

Sources

American Institute of Architects. 1993.
Environmental Resource Guide.
Washington, D.C. April.

Anderson, Cheri. 1994. "Composting: The
Hottest Trend in Recycling." *Recycling
Review*. 3.1: 1.

Arizona Public Service. 1994. *Strategies,
Categories, and Technologies (SCATs)*.
Report. Phoenix, AZ.

Becker, Craig. 1994. "Wellness in the Built
Environment." *Recycling Review*. 2.4: 8–9.

Center for Resourceful Building Technology.
1992. *Carpeting: Indoor Air Quality
Concerns*. Report. Missoula, MT.

Curran, Mary Ann. 1994. "Life Cycle
Assessment." *U.S. Green Building
Conference—1994*. Washington, DC:
Government Printing Office.

EcoGroup, Inc., and Center for Resourceful
Building Technology. 1993. *Design Issues
Guide: Arizona Public Service Company's
Environmental Showcase Home*. Phoenix, AZ.

Mundy, Bruce. 1994. *Indoor Air Pollution:
Solving the Problem*. Term paper, Arizona
State University.

Rossi, Chris. 1994. "Eco-Smart Builders Cut
Down on Building Waste." *Recycling
Review* 2.4: 3.

Spencer, Jon, et al. "Background Radioactivity in
Selected Areas of Arizona and
Implications for Indoor Radon Levels."
*Arizona Geological Survey Open-File
Reports 88-11 and 88-12*. Tucson, AZ:
Arizona Geological Survey.

Stuhr, Kelly. 1993. Physicist's Report from
Radiation Safety Engineering, Inc.
Chandler, AZ.

U.S. Environmental Protection Agency. 1991.
"Radon-Resistant Construction
Techniques for New Residential
Construction, Technical Guidance." Doc.
EPA/625/2–91/032. Washington, D.C.

Wilson, Alex. 1993. "Cellulose Insulation."
Environmental Building News. 2.5:
1/12–16.

5

Sustainable Design

The Environmental Showcase Home combines technologies, materials, and design strategies that, if duplicated in other homes, could lead to an advance in sustainable living in the Southwest. Sustainable living means that what we do today does not deplete resources for the future. We must live on the "interest" of our resources and not on their "principal." Our decisions and choices should insure that future generations can live as comfortably as we do, with sufficient reserves to meet their needs.

In building a home with sustainable building practices, the ESH project team followed the guidelines of *reuse, reduce,* and *recycle* to provide performance standards by which environmentally sound choices could be made concerning home design elements, building materials, and energy and water systems. The ESH demonstrates that technologies are currently available that meet the challenges of resource efficiency, water conservation, and energy reduction and that renewable resources such

as solar energy can be used to reduce the need for more energy-production sources. Through the showcasing of such products and technologies, APS hopes to create an expanded public interest in the production of resource and energy-efficient homes.

This chapter ends with a discussion of the environmental impact of saving energy. Independent research has shown that the energy saved by the design and technologies of the ESH could result in a significant savings in air

Opposite page: **Roof of ESH**

**Decision-making
process based on
principles of
sustainability**

pollution if used by homebuilders throughout the Valley. An epilogue examines site design issues related to the use of ESH principles in larger developments.

Sustainable Development

The concept of sustainable development may be the most important legacy of the environmental movement of the 1970s. Its growth can be traced through three important international conferences that addressed global change in the environment. In 1972 the United Nations Conference on the Human Environment in Stockholm marked the first time international attention was given to pollution's impact on the earth's resources. By bringing these problems to the forefront of public consciousness, the conference encouraged an ongoing dialogue among nations.

Ten years later, the World Commission on Environment and Development met and published *Our Common Future*. In it, the term "sustainable development" was used to describe the balance that we must achieve between environmental savings and economic development: "We must find a way to meet the needs of the present without compromising the ability of future generations to meet their own needs." This declaration makes clear the connection between present resource use and future environmental challenges.

In 1992 the United Nations Conference on Environment and Development was held in Rio de Janeiro. In their publication, *Earth Summit '92*, the participants laid out an agenda that the nations of the world must follow if they are to sustain their natural resources for the future. Though controversies abounded, international political agreement was achieved on many issues. In the book's introduction, UN Secretary-General Boutros Boutros-Ghali claimed that "the Earth Summit . . . marked an important milestone in awakening the world to the need for a development process that does not jeopardize future generations."

These principles of sustainability voiced internationally need to be applied at the local level before they can take effect. Several leading architects and designers have accepted this challenge and have incorporated ideals of sustainable development into their designs of homes and communities. In an article in *Progressive Architecture*, architect Sim Van der Ryn hopes that "the 1990s, through necessity, design, and changing values, will usher in an era of environmentally conscious, sustainable architecture." California landscape architect John Lyle, author of the award-winning book *Design for Human Ecosystems* (1985), also stresses the role of design in saving resources: "We must learn to design natural communities that work with people, in our backyards and in our urban parks and in our industrial developments."

The relationship between sustainability and home design points to the main purpose of the ESH. It is true that the project concerns the design and construction of only one home in one southwestern city. But if the strategies, materials, and design ideas of this singular home can be transferred to several million new homes, then the movement toward the goals of sustainability will be significant.

A guideline of environmental sustainability is that the use of a resource cannot surpass the replacement of that resource. The harvesting of lumber offers an example of the consequences

of disregarding this guideline. Much of the lumber used today is from old-growth forests that provide ecosystem support for numerous plants and animals. Once destroyed, this ecosystem will take several generations to be replenished. Old-growth forests also absorb carbon dioxide, reducing the amount that reaches the upper atmosphere. Because excess carbon dioxide emissions contribute to the greenhouse effect, or the growing warming trend of the earth, the loss of old-growth forest may do irreparable harm to the environment. Finding alternative ways to meet our lumber requirements would contribute to the sustainability of our forest system and narrow the gap between the immediate costs and the true long-term costs of our use of wood. In the ESH, the project team's solutions included the use of lumber from fast-growing trees planted specifically for commercial use and the use of engineered wood to replace solid-sawn lumber. These and other solutions to the use of unsustainable resources, if adopted widely in home construction, could enhance the ideals of sustainability.

Finding a solution to the problem of sustainability depends on our ability to

Our Homes, Ourselves

The APS Environmental Showcase Home illustrates that the sustainability of our planet begins at home. To create a sustainable future, we must meet our current housing needs while also ensuring that resources will be available for future generations to meet their needs.

A sustainable future begins with acknowledging that our households are connected with the earth's natural processes. Each house has a foundation, constructed of materials from the earth. A frame rises from that foundation, built of plant material or metal and covered with wood, bricks, or other natural substances from the ground.

Materials flow into our homes from the living landscape. Water, energy, food, tools, clothing—the necessities of human life—all need to be regenerated. Without an adequate supply of high-quality water, energy to warm and cool us, and food to sustain our bodies, we perish.

Wastes flow out of our homes, created by the production of energy or left over from the amenities of our dwellings. Such wastes are shipped to places often unknown or unacknowledged by those who produce them. Much of what we currently call "waste" could be viewed as a valuable resource if conserved and reused.

If we and our neighbors take too much from our surroundings or put out too much of the wrong character, the environment is degraded. Little by little, small individual decisions concerning our homes combine to have deleterious, cumulative consequences. So we should ask about the sources of our foundations and walls, our food and clothing, our heating and cooling, as well as our packaging and tools. We should be curious as to where our wastes go. And like the Environmental Showcase Home, our homes should be built within our means. The ability of future generations to live and prosper depends on it.

Frederick Steiner
Director, School of Planning and Landscape Architecture
Arizona State University

Actions toward environmental sustainability

- Practice pollution prevention
- Minimize environmental health risks
- Use renewable over nonrenewable resources
- Reuse, reduce, recycle materials
- Use embodied energy in existing material
- Protect endangered resources
- Enhance ecosystem viability
- Minimize water and energy use
- Protect old-growth forests
- Reduce resource deletion rates
- Replace toxic substances in manufacturing processes
- Make use of life cycle assessments

Sustainable design strategies in the ESH

Site
- Hazard-free (radon-free) site
- Indigenous plants
- Site material reuse
- Use of natural topography of site
- Low-maintenance landscaping
- Damaged area restoration
- Restriction of heat-absorbing materials
- Restriction of pesticide and chemical use
- Shade from existing plants

Materials
- Resource efficient
- Low in embodied energy
- High in recycled content
- Nontoxic material
- Recyclable
- No indoor air pollution
- No use of old-growth timber
- No need for finishes
- Natural material in furnishings
- On-site waste reuse
- Material reduction through design
- Use of local products

Water
- Low-flow fixtures
- Low-water-use appliances
- Gray water reuse
- Underground irrigation
- Rainwater harvesting
- Xeriscape
- Hydrozones
- Run-off design
- Retention areas

Energy
- Energy-efficient appliances
- High-efficiency space cooling/heating systems
- Zonal control
- Natural ventilation
- Photovoltaics
- Airtight construction
- Low-energy lighting
- Sun-tempered design
- High-efficiency fenestration
- Shading systems
- Superinsulation
- Low window-to-floor space ratio
- East-west orientation

Environmental benefits

- Indigenous plant preservation
- Reduced chemicals in groundwater
- Fewer natural resources used
- Less potable water used
- Reduced water and wastewater treatment
- Less energy consumed
- Smaller waste stream produced
- Harmful chemicals avoided
- Old-growth forests sustained
- Harmful air emissions avoided
- Landfill life extended

18. Sustainable design strategies

use all our resources more efficiently. To do this, we need to adopt a new sense of environmental stewardship. Our resources of land, energy, water, air, and natural materials will grow more scarce or polluted with each generation if we do not call a halt to our extravagant misuse of them.

Sustainable Design Strategies in the ESH

Figure 18 illustrates how the ideals of sustainability can be advanced through environmentally responsible homebuilding. The figure shows the relationship of the ESH's design strategies to the goals of sustainability and to a number of desired environmental benefits. The number of design strategies of the home, even in this abbreviated list, shows how thoroughly the home's designers and architects thought through the problems of environmentally responsible building. In doing so, they also addressed the larger problems of sustainability, applying solutions at the local level to this global challenge.

The sustainable design strategies of the ESH, as outlined in chapters 2 through 4 of this book, are those that save energy, water, and material resources. The public education strategies are those that will connect the public's environmental ideals with the concept of an environmentally responsible home. If successful, this connection could lead to a marked change in the building of production and custom homes in the Valley.

Energy Savings

The passive solar design of the ESH has three goals: to reduce or avoid the sun's insolation during the summer months, to use it to warm the house during the winter months, and to facilitate the entry of natural light. The home's design strategies and features that save energy include orientation, shading, high R-value insulation, protective window systems, daylighting, and shading devices that result in lowered household energy demand (particularly for cooling).

The application of active technologies together with passive systems can reduce energy use by nearly 60 percent. When photovoltaic applications are added, energy reductions can increase up to 80 percent.

Water Conservation

The ESH shows that through the incorporation of advanced water-saving features and appliances, water use in homes can be curtailed without disrupting family life and comfort. The ESH demonstrates that water savings of around 55 percent can be achieved by installing water-saving technologies indoors and a drought-tolerant landscape outdoors. The gray water system, when operational, can result in total independence from municipal potable water for landscape irrigation. Appliances that use less water also use less energy to heat the water, resulting in multiple benefits.

Resource Efficiency

The ESH demonstrates that resource reduction can be achieved through correct building practices and by selecting the right building materials. Using less construction material for specified structures in the home was one way to help achieve resource reduction. Another was using a light roof made from recycled metal products, which required less structural support. The reuse of construction wastes during the building of the ESH saved material that would have

Regional design strategies address the problems of building in the southwestern desert

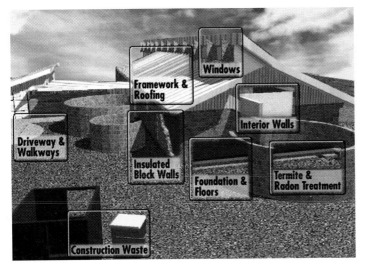

Interactive video showcases environmental aspects of the home

otherwise gone to a landfill. Many products were selected because of their low embodied energy and recycled content.

The project team recognized the need for a sustainable use of resources. The members of the team selected engineered wood products, rather than lumber from old-growth forests, and other wood materials made from small, replenishable forests grown especially for commercial lumber.

Other products were made of recycled glass, plastic, and newsprint. Of all building materials used (including the foundation, walls, studs, sheathing, and roofing), 95 percent has at least some recycled content. Approximately 35 percent of all material used in the home is recycled material.

Public Awareness

As explained in chapter 1, APS's ultimate goal for the ESH was to create a new market for environmentally responsible homebuilding. To reach their target audience of home builders and home buyers, officials in APS's marketing department have planned tours and open houses for consumers, builders, and trade allies in order to let them see how resource and energy efficiency are possible in building today's homes. They have set up displays in the garage of the home that demonstrate the design, materials, and systems used throughout. Cutouts in the home's walls and ceilings show some of the innovative systems that can be used in future homebuilding. An interactive video developed by APS uses computer graphics (a few of which illustrate this book) to help the public understand various facets of the home. These methods of increasing public awareness of the benefits of environmental efficiency are designed to show the public how sustainable design can be achieved using today's homebuilding technology.

The Environmental Impact of Saving Energy

The ESH has been designed to operate with substantially less energy than would a conventional home of similar size. These savings, a result of energy-efficient architecture, materials, appliances, and equipment, will conserve natural resources and reduce the environmental impacts of electrical generation at power plants and throughout the energy supply system. Lower energy use will reduce future air pollution emissions, diminish water use, and lead to less land disruption.

How much environmental benefit can we expect from the ESH's reduced energy requirements alone? Dr. Martin Pasqualetti of ASU, one of the country's leading energy geographers, used energy demand forecasts developed for the ESH by Energy Simulation Specialists of Tempe, Arizona, to determine the amount of air pollutants avoided by the home's reduced use of energy.

Power plants are air polluters. In 1992, electricity generation in the United States produced 15.3 million tons of sulfur dioxide, 7.8 million tons of nitrogen oxide, and 1.8 million tons of carbon dioxide and other contaminants. Over the period 1940–1987, electric utilities were responsible for about 65 percent of the country's sulfur dioxide emissions. The reduction of energy use through energy-efficient design, systems, appliances, and materials will result in decreases of air-polluting emissions at the generating plants and of adverse effects through the entire fuel cycle.

Figure 19 compares the impact on air emissions by the energy consumed in a 2,000-square-foot, energy-inefficient, traditional home versus the ESH. An energy-inefficient home in Phoenix would typically use around 15,700 kWh of electricity per year, while the ESH, with its solar technologies, will use around 3,000 kWh/year. Based on the APS fuel mix and pollution control technologies, we can discern the amount of air pollution released by the generation of energy for each type of home: for every kWh of electricity used, the power plants emit .0030 pounds of sulfur dioxide, .0038 pounds of nitrogen oxide, .0002 pounds of suspended particulates, and 1.62 pounds of carbon dioxide.

The traditional energy-inefficient home then is responsible for 12.8 tons of air pollutants per year from APS's power-generating plants. In contrast, the ESH with its solar energy features is responsible for a mere 2.5 tons per year, avoiding nearly 10 tons of air pollution every year.

A complicating factor in deriving the air emission impacts of reduced energy use is that emission rates of power plants vary by quality of fuel, type, and age of generation equipment, pollution control devices, regional emission standards, and fuel mix. Coal-dependent

Defining the Environmental Showcase Home

The marketing of "greenness" or anything "eco" suffers a significant credibility gap in the minds of consumers. Indeed, the claims of some advertisers, labelers, and marketers regarding the environmental benefits of their products and processes have become scandalous. We at APS recognized early on that it was not enough to say that the ESH was environmentally responsible and energy-efficient. Our claims needed validation from respected research institutions and professionals, and we proceeded to obtain the necessary research and testing.

First, I think it is important to define the ESH. It is not the most environmentally conscious home, nor the most energy-efficient, but it offers a blend of environmental and energy-reducing technologies and design concepts that represent a middle ground worthy of consideration in the marketplace. The application of any combination of the home's features can make a difference—even a significant difference—from an environmental standpoint and with some reasonable economics to boot.

When we joined Region IX of the Environmental Protection Agency and the Arizona Department of Environmental Quality to form the Arizona Environmental Strategic Alliance, we found a great deal of common interest and enthusiasm in the planning and design of the ESH. Personnel from these organizations, along with recognized professionals in the Phoenix area and elsewhere in Arizona and the United States, served on advisory boards and working groups to review and comment on the home's design, materials, energy systems, and site planning. The ESH represents an evolutionary process in decision-making, utilizing local and national expertise. The ESH demonstrates that homes can be built to stringent environmental criteria—resource efficiency, energy conservation, water reduction, high recyclable content, materials reduction, and limited waste—while still providing family comfort, aesthetics, and a quality lifestyle.

Terry Hudgins
Program Leader, Environmental, Health and Safety Initiatives
Arizona Public Service

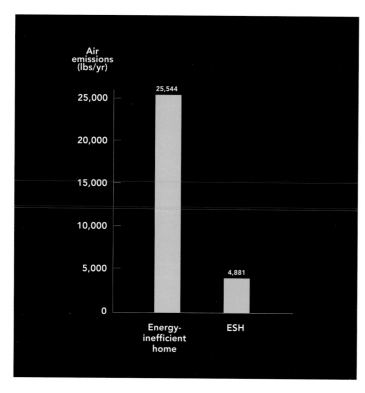

Air
emissions
(lbs/yr)

25,544

25,000

20,000

15,000

10,000

5,000

4,881

0

Energy-
inefficient
home

ESH

**19. Air emissions
comparison**

power plants, for example, reduce their emissions as a result of lower energy use more than do plants that depend on hydropower or other low-polluting energy sources. Because APS has installed highly efficient emission control devices and relies on nuclear power for a sizable portion of its energy needs, its air emission rates are less than average. So it can be seen that, based on the nation's average emission rates, if the ESH were built outside Arizona and compared to a traditional home nearby, it would reduce annual air emissions from 20.7 tons to 3.9 tons per year.

"The total environmental benefits of energy-demand reductions in single-family homes," states Pasqualetti, "are identified more completely by extrapolating the per-home reduced emissions to all the homes permitted in the Phoenix metropolitan area in one year." In 1993, 22,226 new single-family homes were constructed in the area. If all these 1993 homes had been constructed with ESH energy standards, then we could have avoided approximately 207,000 tons of air pollutants!

And if each one of us became environmentally responsible in just home energy use, the avoidance of air emissions from power-generating plants would be enormous. When the indirect and intangible benefits such as visibility, aesthetics, and health are added to the equation, the benefits of homes built nationwide on ESH standards could result in a revolutionary improvement in environmental quality.

The small 2,640-square-foot environmental home at the corner of 60th Street and Greenway in Phoenix makes a large statement. It demonstrates that not only can we build exciting and comfortable homes, but we have the technologies now to become environmentally responsible through our choices in home purchases, home retrofitting, and homebuilding. When environmentally responsible homebuilding becomes the standard, the potential for achieving a sustainable future will be much, much closer.

Sources

Doxsey, W. Laurence. "The City of Austin Green Builder Program." *U.S. Green Building Conference—1994*. Washington, DC: Government Printing Office.

Gordon, Harry T. 1994. "The American Institute of Architects Committee on the Environment." *U.S. Green Building Conference—1994*. Washington, DC: Government Printing Office.

Hill, James E. 1994. "The NIST Green Building Program." *U.S. Green Building Conference—1994*. Washington, DC: Government Printing Office.

Mayo, Tim. 1994. "Canada's Advanced Houses Program." *U.S. Green Building Conference—1994*. Washington, DC: Government Printing Office.

Millhone, John P. 1994. "Green Buildings: DOE's Historical Role and New Directions." *U.S. Green Building Conference—1994*. Washington, DC: Government Printing Office.

Pasqualetti, Martin. Interview with David Pijawka. 10 July 1994.

Thompson, J. William. 1991. "Landscape Design as if Survival Mattered." *Landscape Architecture*. June: 84.

United Nations Conference on Environment and Development. 1993. *Earth Summit 1992*. London: Regency Press.

Van der Ryn, Sim. 1991. "Eco-Villages: Toward Sustainable Architecture." *Progressive Architecture*. 3: 88.

Van der Ryn, Sim, and Peter Calthorpe. 1986. *Sustainable Communities*. San Francisco: Sierra Club.

Weintraub, Deborah. 1994. "Canada's Ten Advanced Houses." *Proceedings of the Sustainable Building Conference*. Los Angeles: Construction Specifications Institute.

World Commission on Environment and Development. 1987. *Our Common Future*. New York: Oxford University Press.

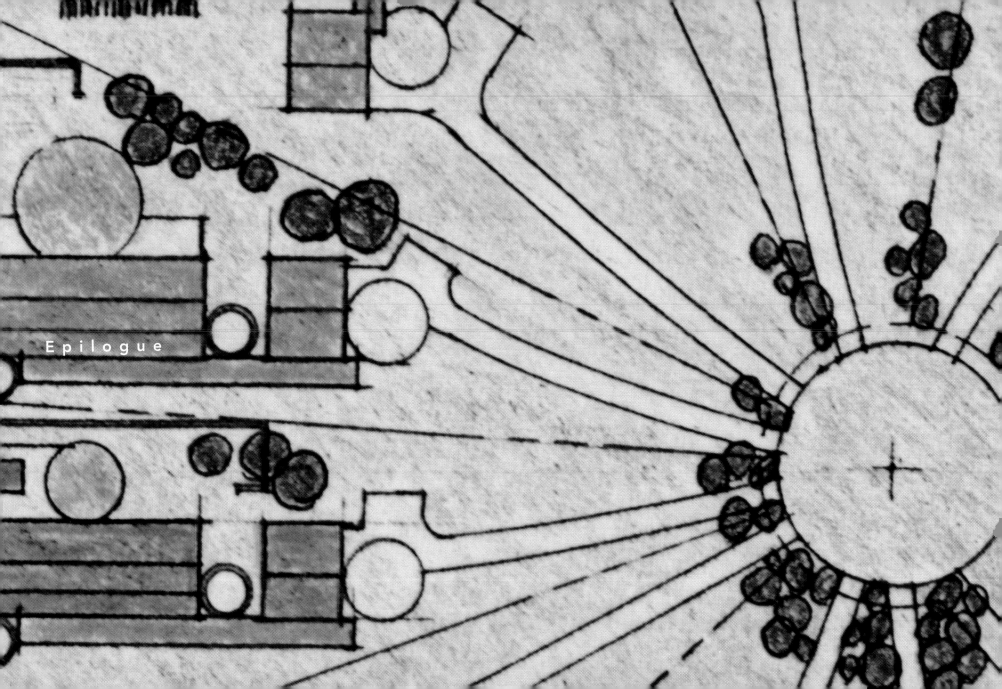

Epilogue

The Next Step: Prototypical Subdivision Design

One environmental showcase home cannot solve our resource and energy problems. It will be necessary to repeat the lessons learned from this project in many homes and subdivisions before we will be able to see a difference in the overall quality of the environment. To answer the question of how this home design could be replicated many times over to become a subdivision, the project team consulted with Michael Underhill, professor and director of the School of Architecture at ASU's College of Architecture and Environmental Design and an expert in urban form. He determined several possible lot layouts that would accomplish different densities of environmentally sensitive homes like the ESH.

The essence of the ESH's design is its east-west orientation and its linear floor plan, which must have the living areas facing south. This constraint presents a challenge for subdivision design, which typically calls for houses to face the street, with the street alignment based on historical and functional factors that have more to do with traffic movement than with home orientation. Underhill addressed this fundamental problem and came up with three development densities that could accommodate the ESH with minor design changes. Figures 20 and 21 depict the three different densities based on the number of homes per acre.

Opposite page:
Illustrative subdivision site plan

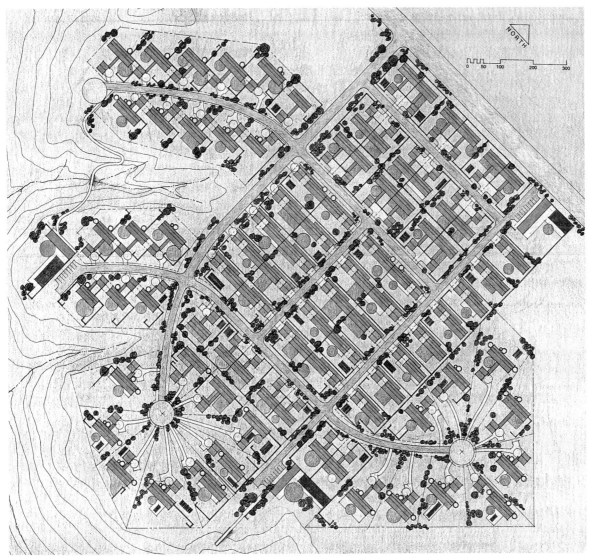

20. Illustrative sub-division site plan

The first area (marked as number 3 in figure 21) has fairly low densities with an average lot size of approximately three-quarters of an acre. Because the lots are large, there are benefits from being able to site the houses on odd-shaped lots and around natural features. Underhill notes that the design of the home lends itself to interesting arrangements at this low density:

> The basic bar of the house runs from east to west, and facing to the south stays constant, but it can be located essentially anywhere on a given lot. The garage wall elements, trellises, and covered entry can be placed in a wide variety of locations on all four sides of the home to adapt to the particular conditions of the lot.

The second area (number 2 in figure 21) shows the home in a higher-density layout. The average lot size is four-tenth of an acre, with a zero-lot-line arrangement. In this plan, houses keep the basic east-west orientation and adapt to a variety of lot shapes.

In the third subdivision design (number 1 in figure 21), there are four units per acre, with the homes attached to form duplexes and reduced from four to three bedrooms. To achieve this density and still retain the appropriate solar orientation, the lot size is reduced to 120 feet by 90 feet, the garage and other landscape features are moved, and the private swimming pool is replaced by a community pool. This configuration also includes more pedestrian pathways and a community recreation facility.

A fundamental problem with the ESH is that, in some ways, it is the wrong answer to the question of sustainable design. Single-family detached residences use up too much of one of our most valuable resources—land. It is not only the land use that is wasteful, but also the necessary infrastructure we must build and the air pollutants we must inhale because of the extra miles we must travel every day throughout our spread-out cities. The answer to this problem requires a change in our social thinking that cannot be brought about by the construction of one environmental home.

Underhill took the home as it was designed and made it fit into various lot configurations under different density scenarios, but density considerations and subdivision design factors should have been a part of the ESH design process from the start. The concept, research, design, and construction of the ESH occurred in a short time frame for a project of this size. Only two-and-one-half years passed from project kick-off to the home's grand opening, probably not enough time to get *everything* right. The home, however, exists as a testimony to what can be done if a dedicated and responsive team of individuals sets out to solve a problem.

21. Illustrative subdivision site plan showing various densities

The Future of Housing

With each new house that is built, we give up many things: we give up open space, water purity, air quality, biodiversity, and the nonrenewable fossil fuels used in extracting, processing, transporting and installing the resources used to build the house. Recycled materials, while a relative improvement over some types of building materials made from virgin resources, are not sustainable if we continue to consume them at present rates.

It is possible to build an extremely resource-efficient home that is both comfortable and functional, but large-square-footage, single-family housing is not going to be sustainable for very long.

(From a review of the manuscript of this book, by Steve Loken and Tracy Mumma of the Center for Resourceful Building Technology)

Appendix A

A number of environmental demonstration homes have been built in North America during the last decade. These homes vary widely in their environmental benefits, depending on the major purposes of their builders. For example, some of the homes are built with affordability as a goal, while others are very expensive, some are built primarily with the theme of sustainability, using recycled or reusable materials, while still others are built primarily to demonstrate new technological advances or products.

One of the oldest environmental demonstration homes is the "Rocky Mountain Institute" in Snowmass, Colorado (16 miles west of Aspen). Completed in January 1984, the 4,000-square-foot structure was designed by Steven Conger and the Aspen Design Group and built by Amory B. and L. Hunter Lovins. Between 1984, when it was first opened to the public, and 1991, the Institute had received over 25,000 visitors. The structure provides a combined living space for institute members, staff, and their guests, office space for the research center, and a year-round space for growing fruits, vegetables, flowers, and fish. The home was designed to address five crucial sustainability issues: energy, water, agriculture, security, and economic renewal. The building is almost totally dependent on solar energy for electricity and water heating, drawing only about 10 percent of the normal dwelling's amount of public utility-provided electricity, and uses less than half of a normal dwelling's potable water consumption.

Some of the demonstration homes, of course, are more innovative than others. One example of a futuristic concept is the "earth ship" design of architect Michael Reynolds of Taos, New Mexico. Described as "visionary" in a *New York Times* article in 1993, Reynolds's earth ships are constructed from old tires stuffed with dirt (a variation of rammed-earth technology). The unusual homes are considered pleasant in appearance and feature horseshoe-shaped rooms and well-lit hallways with large windows of solar panels. The earth ship homes also feature rooftop snow and rainwater catchment systems, gray water plant irrigation for interior wetlands (much like a greenhouse, where both plants and food crops are raised), and photovoltaic cells for electricity. Reynolds is currently building a self-sustaining community of some two to three hundred earth ships in an area about 15 miles west of Taos.

An innovative use of recycled materials can be found in the "Resource Conservation Research House" (also popularly referred to as the "Garbage House"), in Bowie, Maryland. Built by the National Association of Home Builders to educate its members and consumers, this 3,600-square-foot home with four bedrooms and two baths opened in December 1992. It is made entirely from recycled products and is designed to conserve energy. Some examples of innovative building concepts include steel frame construction salvaged from automobile junkyards and dismantled bridges, siding made from sawmill wastes and wood chips, and insulation composed of recycled polystyrene. Some of the electricity conservation methods include solar panels, photovoltaic cells, and a heat pump system with buried copper piping to make use of the earth's own heating and cooling.

Another innovative approach to environmental homes was taken by Martin Liefhebber and Myrna Moore, architects of the "Codicile House" in Toronto, Canada. (The unique name for the project was formed from a combination of "codicil," because the house is designed as an adjunct to the main house, and "domicile," because it is a residence.) The explicit goal of this project was to produce an affordable two-bedroom home with technology that would allow it to be independent of city utilities. Therefore, the three-story, 800-square-foot house has its own energy and water supply, sewage disposal system, and rooftop greenhouse. Three-quarters of a cord of wood can completely heat the home and only one cup of water flushes the composting toilet. Key features include solar panels, thermopiles, and a soapstone wood stove for electricity production; a foaming-compost toilet; a refuse-to-composting tank; a gray water reuse system; rainwater collection for drinking purposes; and new innovations like cellulose-block construction.

Canada has taken a very forward-looking approach to promoting sustainable building. The national Advanced Houses Program, administered by CANMET, the Canada Centre for Mineral and Energy Technology, and the Canadian Home Builders' Association, cosponsored a national competition for houses that minimize housing impact on the environment and provide improved indoor air quality. Eleven houses in eight provinces (three in Ontario, two in Quebec, and one each in Manitoba, British Columbia, Saskatchewan, Nova Scotia, New Brunswick, and Prince

Edward Island) were selected for the program. One of these demonstration/ research homes is the "Waterloo Green Home" in Waterloo, Ontario, which was opened to the public in April 1993. Designed by architect Richard Reichard and built by Enermodal Engineering as a prototype home, it includes among other features a macerating toilet and a prototype hand-built furnace developed by Canada Gas. Another Canadian home, the "Advanced House" in Vancouver, British Columbia, was completed in June 1993. Under the direction of architect Richard Kadulski, the demonstration home was targeted toward builders and consumers to spur national research and development in resource-responsive, environmentally sensitive building.

A home designed specifically to demonstrate the use of recycled, reused, and nontoxic materials for home construction is the "GreenHouse" in Pierce County, Washington. Completed in September 1993, the 43 by 27-foot exhibit is constructed of modular elements. It is also a reusable, mobile teaching facility designed to demonstrate a "closing the recycling loop" philosophy.

Another showcase home is the King County "Home for the Holidays" demonstration project which opened in 1993. This home contains many of the features usually found in environmental demonstration homes, namely energy-conserving features such as double-glazed windows, exterior roll shutters, clerestory windows, sun room, and trees for shade; water-conserving techniques including low-flush toilets and a front-loading washer; and electricity-conserving techniques such as fluorescent lighting and a microwave oven. However, the key feature and primary interest in the "Home for the Holidays" is the amount of recycled material used in construction (i.e., carpets, paint, ceiling insulation, worm bin, and food burial system).

In Tucson, Arizona, "GreenHome 21" was designed by Seaver Franks Architects and constructed by Homes by Herder, Inc. Designed to appeal to upscale buyers of the 1990s, the home is billed as the first environmentally sensitive, energy- and resource-efficient, automated home. It will not be open to the public on a regular basis. A fully automated system will be operated by remote controls, keyboards, phones, or personal computers to control the heating, cooling, security, entertainment, and lighting systems. The home also includes a gray water collection system to funnel 90 gallons of reusable water per day to the desert landscaping.

Recently completed in Tucson, Arizona, is a home designed to fill the needs of a different economic group. The Desert Home was built by the Tucson Urban League to provide affordable housing while also conserving natural resources. The Desert Home uses only systems that are low in cost to install and maintain, and is designed for maximum owner participation in the building process.

Another environmental demonstration home in Arizona is located in the Desert Botanical Garden in Phoenix. The guiding philosophy for the house, which opened in May 1993, was to present technology, equipment strategies, and materials that can be used to build an environmentally sensitive home at a reasonable price. The energy-saving features used in the home include heavier insulation, double-glazed windows, and a heat pump. Additional landscape shade and water savings accrue from low-water-use appliances and fixtures. Passive solar technology is incorporated for water heating and courtyard lighting.

Another of the showcase homes is the "New American Home for 1993" in Las Vegas, Nevada, designed by architect Jan Van Tilberg. This home was intended to demonstrate several goals: use of futuristic information technology (such as library access and a media center), provisions and applications for handicapped persons, use of recycled materials, and conservation of energy used for heating and cooling.

The "E3 (Energy Efficient Environment) Home" in California was built by a public/private partnership of the Building Industrial Association of Superior, the California Energy Commission, and Pacific Gas and Electric. The home's objective was to reduce energy use by up to 70 percent. The "E3 Home" has some automated features such as computer control of appliances, lighting, and security. This home emphasizes good indoor air quality by using a controlled fresh-air ventilation system.

The "National ReCRAFT 90" house located in western Montana was completed in the spring of 1992. The house was built by the Center for Resourceful Building Technology of Missoula, Montana, to demonstrate building products and systems that exemplify the efficient use of resources. Specific emphasis is placed on the heating system and basement, as well as on the use of recycled materials and decreased use of virgin timber. The 2,400-square-foot residence is bermed into a hillside to reduce heat loss and includes an innovative cooling tower. The home is designed to meet three expressed goals: resource and energy efficiency, water conservation, and indoor air quality. The target audience for the home is builders, architects, and the public.

The "Good Cents Home" located in Jackson, Georgia, (a suburb of Atlanta) was not built as an environmental home demonstrating energy-saving features, but was funded by *Southern Living* magazine as an "idea" home. The home, which opened in July 1993, was built by the Jackson Electric Membership Corporation. The enthusiastic response to this prototype home has spurred Jackson Electric to begin work on a geothermal subdivision of thirty-three homes.

Another home not built specifically for sustainability is the "Eco-Smart Home" of Victor, New York (a suburb of Rochester). Built by the Archer Group, this home is sponsored by the Eco Design Builders who put on one "Eco-Smart" demonstration home each year for the local Parade of Homes. The 1994 theme was "Health House." ("Energy Efficiency" and "Total Efficiency" were themes in previous years.)

The "Advance Green Builder Home" in Austin, Texas, is scheduled for completion in January 1995. Built by the Public Research & Education Center for Maximum Potential Building Systems, this home is the result of another public/private partnership between the local gas company (Austin Electric) and the Capital Area Builders Association. Key features of the Advance Green Builder Home include new product development (particularly coal combustion byproducts), the reuse of the entire wastewater supply, and a living fence to surround the one-acre lot.

The trend of the last decade toward incorporating concepts of sustainability into building construction has not been limited to the residential arena alone. Just recently, WalMart began construction of a new "Eco-Mart" in Lawrence, Kansas. Designed by BSW Architects of Tulsa, Oklahoma, the new Eco-Mart will feature exterior masonry walls for durability and thermal storage capacity, a system of skylights and dimmable fluorescent lighting fixtures, roof trusses produced from sustainably harvested timber, and a recycled stormwater irrigation system.

The following table lists selected environmental homes and explains their key features.

Name	Location	Architect/Builder	Key Features
United States			
Advance Green Builder Home	Austin, Texas	Public Research and Education Center for Maximum Potential Building Systems	Emphasizes new product development (particularly coal consumption byproducts). Waste water reuse. Living fence.
Desert Home	Tucson, Arizona	Corky Poster Tucson Urban League	Affordable housing for low- and moderate-income home buyers. Self-help construction with owner participation. Duplex, 3-bedroom. High-mass construction. Energy-efficient and low-water-use appliances.
Desert House	Phoenix, Arizona	Salt River Project	Passive solar water heater. Low-water-use appliances. Rainwater catchment for landscaping use. On-site family occupation for demonstration/research/ observation purposes. "Rumford" radiant heat fireplace.
E3 (Energy Efficient Environment)	California	Building Industrial Assn. of Superior	Controlled fresh-air ventilation system. Computer-automated appliances, lighting and security systems. Up to 70 percent reduction in energy use.
Earth Ships	Taos, New Mexico	Michael Reynolds	Building blocks of tires filled with dirt. Photovoltaic cells for electricity generation. Rooftop catchment system for harvesting rain and snow. Gray water reuse system. Indoor wetlands for food production.
Eco-Smart Home	Victor, New York	The Archer Group Eco Design Builders	One of a series of theme homes for annual Parade of Homes. 1990s themes include energy efficiency, total efficiency, and health.
Good Cents Home	Jackson, Georgia	Jackson Electric Membership Corp.	Funded as "idea" home for geothermal power generation.

Name	Location	Architect/Builder	Key Features
United States (cont.)			
GreenHome 21	Tucson, Arizona	Seaver Franks Architects Homes by Herder, Inc.	User-friendly automated heating, cooling, security, entertainment, and lighting systems. Gray water collection system for irrigation.
The GreenHouse	Pierce County, Washington	Stafford Architect	Recycled and nontoxic building materials. Modular construction for mobility as teaching facility. Prototype CFC-free refrigerator.
Home for the Holidays	King County		Recycled materials (carpet, carpet pads, paint, insulation). Fluorescent lighting. Low-water-use toilets, clothes washer. Passive solar system.
New American Home for 1993	Las Vegas, Nevada	Jan Van Tilberg, Architect Lewis Homes of Nevada	Recycled building materials.Futuristic technology, including library and media center. Applications for handicapped occupants. Minimal energy costs.
ReCRAFT 90	Missoula, Montana	Center for Resourceful Building Technology	Decreased use of virgin timber. Recycled materials. Heating system and cooling tower.
Resource Conservation Research House (Garbage House)	Bowie, Maryland	National Association of Home Builders	Built from recycled material (steel framing from junkyards and dismantled bridges, siding from sawmill wastes and wood chips. insulation from recycled polystyrene). Solar panels and photo-voltaic cells for electricity generation. Heat pump with buried copper piping.
Rocky Mountain Institute	Snowmass, Colorado	Steven Congers, The Aspen Design Group Amory B. Lovins and L. Hunter Lovins	Provides 4,000 square feet of residential and office space. Almost total reliance on solar technology for electricity generation. Half of normal potable water use. Growing space for fruits, vegetables, fish, and flowers.

Name	Location	Architect/Builder	Key Features
Canada			
British Columbia Advanced House	Surrey, British Columbia	Richard Kadulski, Architect	Recycled glass and crushed-stone site drainage. Innovative cement/cellulose composite roof and floor tiles. Non-CFC-polyurethane insulation. Automation system.
Codicile House	Toronto, Ontario	Martin Liefhebber and Myrna Moore	Affordable. Independent from city utilities. Energy from solar panels, thermopile, and soapstone wood stove. Water conservation: rainwater collection for drinking, compost toilet, refuse-compost tank, gray water system. Cellulose-block construction.
Envirohome	Bedford, Nova Scotia	Dick Miller Clayton Developments	Solar hot water with photovoltaic pump. Heat-recovery system. Demand-control ventilation system with relative humidity sensors. Radiant heat fireplace. Recycled building materials. Automation system.
Innova House	Kanata, Ontario	Bruce Gough Energy Building Group	Photovoltaics for lighting and/or heat recovery ventilator. Cistern for rainwater storage. Prototype sealed-combustion gas range and clothes dryer. Prototype non-CFC phenolic board insulation. 94 percent efficiency-integrated gas heating/domestic hot water .
Maison, Novtec	Montreal, Quebec	Robert Booth Hansed Booth Building Science and Technology	Exterior "outsulation" sandwich walls. Ground-source heat pump with water and air distribution loops. Plastic-fiber wall insulation made from recycled plastic bottles. Recycled material for roofing. Composting toilet.
Maison Performante	Laval, Quebec	Hugh Ward l'Association provinciale des constructeurs d'habitations du Quebec	Passive solar with solarium. Closed loop heat pump. Solar water heating. Insulation "glass blocks." Automation system.

Name	Location	Architect/Builder	Key Features
Canada (cont.)			
Manitoba Advanced House	Winnipeg, Manitoba	Don Galys Manitoba Home Builders Association	Gray water heat recovery and attic air recirculation for water preheat. Recycled glass and crushed-stone site drainage. High-density mesh solar-shade windowscreens. Sump pump/cistern water collection system for land-scaping use. Separately ventilated smoking and hobby room.
The Neat Home	Hamilton, Ontario	Don Buchan Buchan, Lawton, and Parent	Integrated heating/hot water/ventilation/heat recovery system. Rainwater collection system. Low-flow plumbing fixtures. Use of recycled building materials. Automation system.
New Brunswick Advanced House	Frederictown, New Brunswick	Hazen Spinney Spinney's Housing and Construction, Ltd.	Ground-source heat pump. Radiant collection system. Heat recovery ventilator. Passive solar system with in-ground storage tanks.
P.E.I. Advanced House	Charlottetown, Prince Edward Island	Norman Finlayson	Ground-source heat pump. Photovoltaic cells to generate electricity. Wind turbine and tower. Quadruple-glazed windows with reflecting film. Airfill and insulation.
Saskatchewan Advanced Technology House	Saskatoon, Saskatchewan	John Carroll Carroll Homes	Ground-source cooling with buried pipe. Photovoltaics for heat recovery ventilation and emergency lighting. Reflecting light "pipes." Prototype sealed-combustion gas range and oven. Prototype gray water heat recovery system. Solar-powered heat-storage tanks.
Waterloo GreenHome	Waterloo, Ontario	Stephen Carpenter Enermodal Engineering Ltd.	Recycled cellulose insulation. Solar hot water with photovoltaic pump. Prototype combination gas furnace/heat recovery ventilator. Extra-low-flush (3-litre) toilet. Prototype sealed-combustion gas stove.

Appendix B

Product	Manufacturer	Functional Area	Environmental Benefits
Sitework			
Dragnet FT	FMC Corporation 1735 Market Street Philadelphia, PA 19103	Preconstruction termite treatment	Least toxic termiticide. Manufactured from water-based pyrethrum. Degrades rapidly in sunlight.
Stabilizer soil stabilizer	Stabilizer 4832 E. Indian School Rd. Phoenix, AZ 85018 (800-336-2468)	Stabilized decomposed granite for driveway	Does not absorb and radiate heat as does concrete. Allows water to penetrate, preventing rainwater runoff. Can be reused if repairs are necessary.
ET 1 Calsense irrigation controller	Calsense 2075 Corte del Nogal, Suite P Carlsbad, CA 92009 (800-572-8608)	Landscape water management	Produces reports on water consumption which aid in water administration. Insures that the correct amount of water is delivered to plants.
Geoflow subsurface irrigation system with ROOTGUARD technology	Geoflow, Inc. 200 Gate 5 Road, #103 Sausalito, CA 94966 (800-828-3388)	Subsurface irrigation	Can cut water consumption by 50 percent compared to surface drip systems. ROOTGUARD technology prevents tree roots from clogging the system.
Vector Flow Line	Vector Irrigation Technologies, Inc. P.O. Box 700095 San Antonio, TX 78270-0095 (210-490-2074)	Lawn irrigation enhancer	Delivers water directly to roots so there is no overspray or evaporation loss. Works well in difficult-to-design water areas and with gray water irrigation.
Waccamaw walkway and patio pavers	Waccamaw Clay Products Co., Inc. 3300 Waccamaw Blvd. Myrtle Beach, SC 29578 (803-236-2121)	Walkway pavers, entryway, exterior of home	Pavers are partially manufactured from soil containing oil residue.
Concrete step-stones	Bowman Concrete 949 W. Birchwood Mesa, AZ 85210 (602-835-1094)	Pathway pavers	Using premanufactured circular cardboard forms speeds and simplifies installation. Can be removed and reused intact.

Product	Manufacturer	Functional Area	Environmental Benefits
Concrete			
Flyash	Various suppliers of concrete mixtures and additives	Replaces 25 percent of portland cement in concrete floors	Strengthens concrete. Produces no off-gassing that could produce air pollution. Lasts the life of the home. Saves flyash, a waste product, from going to landfill. Decreases the amount of high-embodied-energy cement that is used.
Integral color concrete colorants	Various suppliers of concrete mixtures and additives	Provides color for concrete floors	Easy to maintain, attractive. Lasts the life of the home.
Masonry			
Integra concrete masonry	Superlite Block 4150 W. Turney Phoenix, AZ 85019	Most of home's exterior walls	Made of 25 percent flyash. Durable, high thermal storage capacity and insulative value. Serves as both structure and finish. Only one thermal bridge point that conducts heat.
Supergreen Foam insulation	H.C. Fennell, Inc. P.O. Box 87, Route 5 North Thetford, VT 05054 (802-333-4333)	Used with block on exterior wall system	Made with hydrofluorocarbons (HFCs), does not contain chlorine or urea formaldehyde, eliminating ozone-damaging off-gassing. R-6.5 per inch. Overall R-value of wall system is R-24.
Metals			
Recycled content nails and fasteners	Various suppliers, including: W.H. Maze Company 100 Church Street Peru, IL 61354 (815-223-8290)	Nails, screws, fasteners, and connectors used throughout the project	Made from recycled steel. Packaging is from recycled products. Acid and zinc byproducts from production are recyclable.
Reinforcing steel	Various manufacturers	Reinforcing concrete and masonry	High recycled content.

Product	Manufacturer	Functional Area	Environmental Benefits
Wood and Plastics			
Trex composite plastic lumber	Mobil Chemical Company Composite Products Division 800 Connecticut Ave. Norwalk, CT 06856 (800-846-2739)	Siding on house, gates, pool deck, and landscape edging and timbers	Does not require painting or sealant. Made from recycled woods and plastic. Uses no preservatives. Fully recyclable.
Oriented strand board (OSB)	Various manufacturers, including: Potlatch Corp. P.O. Box 3704 Spokane, WA 99220-3704 (509-328-0935)	Roof sheathing, exterior framed walls and garage roof sheathing	Enables use of smaller, faster-growing trees or lumber byproducts that would have been discarded or burned.
Steel studs	American Studco P.O. Box 6633 Phoenix, AZ 85005 (800-877-8823)	Interior wall framing	Replaces traditional wood framing, helping to conserve natural wood resources. Fully recyclable. May contain 60 percent or more recycled content. Can be manufactured to custom lengths so less material is wasted on the job site.
Medite II wood door frame and jambs	Medite Corporation P.O. Box 4040 Medford, OR 97501 (800-676-3339)	Interior door trim and molding, jamb material	No formaldehyde used in manufacturing. Made from saw and milling dust. Highly durable.
Finger-jointed stud framing	Various manufacturers	Exterior framed wall, used in vertical wall studs	Made from small pieces of wood glued together that would have otherwise been discarded or burned. Straighter, stronger, and more stable than a solid piece of lumber.
TJI Joists	Trus Joist MacMillan P.O. Box 60 Boise, ID 83707 (800-628-3997)	Structural framing of roof and ceiling	More efficient use of forest resources than joists made with ordinary lumber. Can be made with smaller, faster-growing trees that are harvested on a sustainable basis.

Product	Manufacturer	Functional Area	Environmental Benefits
Wood and Plastics (cont.)			
Microllam LVL	Trus Joist MacMillan P.O. Box 60 Boise, ID 83707 (800-628-3997)	Facia/subfacia	More efficient use of forest resources than joists made with ordinary lumber. Can be made with smaller, faster-growing trees that are harvested on a sustainable basis.
TimberStrand	Trus Joist MacMillan P.O. Box 60 Boise, ID 83707 (800-628-3997)	Facia/subfacia	Made from smaller, faster-growing trees; no old-growth timber is used. Resource-efficient use of otherwise unusable aspen trees.
Parallam PSL	Trus Joist MacMillan P.O. Box 60 Boise, ID 83707 (800-628-3997)	Main structural support beams and window headers	Made from smaller, faster-growing trees; no old-growth timber is used.
Thermal and Moisture Protection			
RTS Standing Seam Shingles	RTS Company 1805 Newton Avenue San Diego, CA 92113 (800-879-8382)	House and garage roof	Made of 60 percent recycled steel. Fully recyclable. Lowers cooling requirements within house by reflecting sunlight. Reduces roofing weight substantially, thus reducing structural mass of roof framing walls and foundations.
Sola-Tube natural lighting	Sola-Tube 5825 Avenida Encinas #101 Carlsbad, CA 92008 (619-929-6060)	Skylight in entry	80 percent less heat gain than traditional skylights. Helps eliminate the need for electrical lighting.
Mirrorseal Superior Roofing System	Innovative Formulations Corporation 670 West 33rd Street Tucson, AZ 85713 (800-346-7265)	Roofing on low-slope entry canopy roof	Contains no petroleum-based materials. Base, made of saltwater, is nontoxic. Has a solar reflectance of 82 percent, reducing solar gain.

Product	Manufacturer	Functional Area	Environmental Benefits
Thermal and Moisture Protection (cont.)			
Nature Guard cellulose insulation	Louisiana-Pacific 111 SW Fifth Avenue Portland, OR 97204-3601 (503-221-0800)	Blown into framed walls and above ceiling	R-value of 3.8 per inch; less energy needed to heat and cool home. Completely seals wall cavity. Made from recycled newspapers. Nontoxic, nonirritating. Overall R-value of 22 in walls and 38 in ceiling.
Insul-Tray ventilation chutes and radiant barrier panels	Insul-Tray, Inc. 1881 E. Crestview Drive Shelton, WA 98584 (206-427-5930)	Venting of south slope of roof deck	Reduces roof heat gain. Made from 100 percent recycled postconsumer wastepaper.
Air krete cementitious foam insulation	Nordic Builders 162 N. Sierra Court Gilbert, AZ 85234 (602-892-0603)	Insulation in gable-end walls and garage roof and walls	Improves energy efficiency of the home. Nontoxic. R-3.9 per inch. Ozone-safe. No formaldehyde, petroleum, CFCs, or VOCs.
AMOFOAM-RCY Insulation Board	Amoco Foam Products Company 375 Northridge Road, Suite 600 Atlanta, GA 30350 (800-241-4402)	Perimeter slab insulation	High R-value. Made from 50 percent recycled plastic. Contains no CFCs.
AMOFOAM Sill Sealer	Amoco Foam Products Company 375 Northridge Road, Suite 600 Atlanta, GA 30350 (800-241-4402)	Sill sealer at edges of frame walls	Reduces air infiltration. Contains no CFCs.
AMOWRAP Housewrap	Amoco Foam Products Company 375 Northridge Road, Suite 600 Atlanta, GA 30350 (800-241-4402)	Air-infiltration barrier on framed walls	Reduces air infiltration. Contains no CFCs.
Doors and Windows			
Hurd wood windows	Hurd Millwork Company, Inc. 575 Whelen Avenue Medford, WI 54451 (209-832-2219)	Windows throughout the home	Frames are aluminum-clad wood and are durable in desert heat and dryness. Wood used from managed forests. Aluminum frames are recyclable.

Product	Manufacturer	Functional Area	Environmental Benefits
Doors and Windows (cont.)			
Norwood Series 3050 patio door	Fleetwood Aluminum Products, Inc. 2485 Railroad Street Corona, CA 91720 (714-279-1070)	Oversized patio sliding door (the "glass wall")	Aluminum made from recycled products. High R-value.
Superglass system with Heat Mirror film and HeatSeal thermal break spacer	Southwall Technologies 1029 Corporation Way Palo Alto, CA 94303 (800-365-8794)	Glass system used in Hurd windows and in patio sliding door	An R-value of 9 provides 92 percent of the insulative value of a typical wall.
Better-Bilt windows	Better-Bilt Company 7555 Highway 69 Prescott Valley, AZ 86314 (602-772-7000)	Garage sliding windows	Thermally broken aluminum frame. Recyclable. With R-4 insulated glass, design prevents heat transfer, lowering energy costs.
Avanti series doors	Peachtree Doors & Windows P.O. Box 5700 Norcross, GA 30091	Exterior doors for home and garage	High R-value. Door jamb is made from recycled materials and resource-efficient wood.
Interior doors	Executive Door Company Phoenix, AZ (602-272-8076)	Interior doors throughout the home	No formaldehyde used in manufacturing. Made from saw and milling dust. Highly durable, quality and feel of solid-core doors.
Retractable trellis with SheerWeave 4100 fabric	Awnings by Design 15475 N. Greenway-Hayden Loop #12 Scottsdale, AZ 85260 (602-951-9771)	North and south shade structures	Prevents direct sunlight from reaching window glass. Controls solar heat gain.
Fixed awnings and sun sponges with Dixlon 32 textile fiber	Awnings by Design 15475 N. Greenway-Hayden Loop #12 Scottsdale, AZ 85260 (602-951-9771)	East and west shade structures	Prevents direct sunlight from reaching window glass. Controls solar heat gain.
Win-Trol M-2100 window motorizing system	Win-Trol, Inc. P. O. Box 4425 Helena, MT 59604 (406-449-6616)	Clerestory windows	Motorizes skylight for easy opening and closing for air movement.

Product	Manufacturer	Functional Area	Environmental Benefits
Finishes			
Corian surfacing material	DuPont Corian P.O. Box 80702 Wilmington, DE 19898 (800-4CORIAN)	Part of kitchen counter	Uses recycled and postconsumer materials. Production also incorporates postindustrial recycling. Inert and stable. No off-gassing.
Wilsonart plastic laminate	Various suppliers, including: Ralph Wilson Plastics Co. 969 Third Avenue, 4th Floor New York, NY 10022 (800-762-3683)	High-pressure plastic laminate for kitchen counter top	High durability. May contain some recycled newspaper. Minimal plastic used.
Santana POLY-MAR HD countertop	Santana Solid Plastic Products P.O. Box 2021 Scranton, PA 128501	Guest bathroom countertop	Made from 90 percent recycled plastic.
Medite II fiberboard	Medite Corporation P.O. Box 4040 Medford, OR 97501 (800-676-3339)	Substrate/structure for millwork/cabinets in kitchens and bathrooms	No formaldehyde used in manufacturing. Made from saw and milling dust. Highly durable.
Environ fiberboard	Phenix Composites, Inc. P.O. Box 609 Mankato, MN 56002-0609 (800-324-8187)	Cabinet fronts in dining room	Made from recycled newspaper and soy flour. No dioxin is released during production; the newspapers are not de-inked. Natural dyes.
Homasote burlap panels	Homasote Company Box 7240 West Trenton, NJ 08628-0240 (800-257-9491)	Interior wall finish	Made from natural fabric and recycled newsprint. Do not contain asbestos.
USG gypsum wallboard	United States Gypsum Company 125 South Franklin Street Chicago, IL 60680-4124 (818-956-1882)	Wallboard used on the interior finish of painted walls of the home	In some areas of the country, may contain gypsum from other waste streams and may be recyclable. 100 percent recycled face sheets.

Product	Manufacturer	Functional Area	Environmental Benefits
Finishes (cont.)			
The Nailer drywall stop	Millennium Group 121 S. Monroe St. Waterloo, WI 53594 (800-280-2304)	Corner and top plate nailer for drywall	Made from recycled plastic. Reduces studs needed, eliminating thermal bridges and allowing additional insulation to be added.
Plaster stucco base coat	Phoenix Cement Company 2501 W. Behrend Dr., Suite 23 Phoenix, AZ (602-264-0511)	Exterior stucco base coat for wood-framed walls	Base coat contains flyash. Eliminates need for painting or other finishing.
Plaster stucco finish coat	Western Stucco Products Co., Inc. 66101 N. 53rd Dr. Glendale, AZ 85311 (602-937-9141)	Colored finish coats for stucco	Integral color eliminates need for paint now and in future.
Glidden SPRED 2000	Glidden Paint Company Strongville Research Center 16651 Sprague Road Strongville, OH 44136 (800-221-4100)	Interior paint used throughout home	Contains low quantities of preservatives and fungicides and no VOCs. Reduces indoor and outdoor pollution.
AFM Safecoat Hard Seal	American Formulating and Manufacturing 1960 Chicago Ave. E. Riverside, CA 92507 (909-781-6860)	Clear finish on wood	Made in environmentally safe manner. Is nontoxic.
Enviro-Tech carpet	Image Carpets, Inc. P.O. Box 5555 Armuchee, GA 30105 (800-722-2504)	Interior carpet	Made from 100 percent recycled plastic, replacing the need for crude oil, the traditional raw material for carpet.
Chris-Craft Contract Carpet Pad	Chris-Craft Industrial Products Waterford Division P.O. Box 70 Waterford, NY 12188 (800-765-4723)	Padding for carpet	Made from natural jute fiber instead of urethane and rubber. Produces no off-gassing or emission from the pad.
Envirotec Healthguard Adhesives	W.F. Taylor Co., Inc. 11545 Pacific Avenue Fontana, CA 92337 (800-397-4583)	Glue for carpet pad	Nontoxic, low odor and solvent-free. Contain no carcinogenic materials and do not emit any hazardous vapors.

Product	Manufacturer	Functional Area	Environmental Benefits
Finishes (cont.)			
Stoneware Traffic Tile	Stoneware Tile Company Richmond, IN (317-935-4760)	Tile in bathrooms	Made from 70 percent recycled glass from auto windshields.
Armstone Confetti cast marble floor tile	PermaGrain Products, Inc. 13 West Third Street Medina, PA 19063 (215-565-1575)	Kitchen floor tile	Made from twice-recycled marble chips and dust. Damaged or otherwise unacceptable tiles and slabs are recast to create tiles.
Equipment			
Westinghouse LT350R	Frigidaire Company 6000 Perimeter Drive Dublin, OH 43017 (800-245-0600)	Clothes washer	Front load washer: uses 1/3 less water and 1/3 less energy than average top load washer, reducing demand for hot water.
Westinghouse DE350R	Frigidaire Company 6000 Perimeter Drive Dublin, OH 43017 (800-245-0600)	Clothes dryer	Companion to clothes washer selected.
Amana DU7500	Amana Refrigeration Company Amana, IA 52204	Dishwasher	Uses less water than conventional dishwasher. Has a wider variety of temperature settings.
Whirlpool SERP Super Efficient Refrigerator	Whirlpool Home Appliances 2020 E. University Phoenix, AZ 85062 (800-442-1111)	Kitchen refrigerator	Energy-efficient. Uses CFC-free refrigerant.
GE Profile JP393R	General Electric Company 9500 Williamsburg Plaza Louisville, KY 40222 (800-626-2000)	Kitchen induction cooktop	Energy efficient; uses 10 percent less energy than standard equipment. Cooktop remains cool during cooking.
Thermador Convection Micro Thermal Oven, Model CMT-227	Thermador 5119 District Boulevard Los Angeles, CA 90040 (800-758-1001)	Kitchen oven	Energy efficient; uses 30 percent less energy than standard equipment.

Product	Manufacturer	Functional Area	Environmental Benefits
Equipment (cont.)			
Thermos Electric Grill - 1500 watt	Thermos Company Route 75 Freeport, IL 61032 (800-553-6162)	Electric grill	Uses vacuum technology, cutting cooking time and using less energy. No pollution produced.
Furniture			
FoxFibre cotton	Natural Cotton Colours, Inc. P.O. Box 66 Wickenburg, AZ 85358 (602-684-7199)	Fabrics in master bedroom	Fabric is cotton that is grown organically in Arizona. Color is bred into cotton, so that no dyes or other coloring are needed.
Bench swing	Superwood P.O. Box 2399 107 Avenue C Selma, AL (205-874-3781)	Outdoor patio	100 percent recycled postconsumer content. Chemical-free.
Twist lounge chair	meta-morf P. O. Box 40106 Portland, OR 97240 (503-295-2654)	Outdoor patio	99 percent recycled postconsumer plastic.
Folding chairs and umbrella table	Poly-Wood 207 N. Huntington St. Syracuse, IN 46567 (219-457-3284)	Outdoor patio	100 percent recycled postconsumer content.
Sling seat rocker, Ergorondack chair and ottoman	Yemm & Hart RR 1, Box 173 Marquand, MO 63655-9610 (314-783-5434)	Pool area	Constructed from extruded plastic lumber from recycled plastic. All components are recyclable.
Ocarina fabric bedspread	Ocarina Textiles 16 Cliff Street New London, CT 06320 (203-437-8189)	Master bedroom	FoxFibre cotton is woven on a 1920s loom salvaged from a defunct mill.

Product	Manufacturer	Functional Area	Environmental Benefits
Furniture (cont.)			
Mattress	Restonic of Arizona P. O. Box 25488 Phoenix, AZ 85002-5488	Master bedroom	Made from CFC-free foam. Minimal use of materials compared with similar mattresses.
Platform bed frame and mattress	Heart of Vermont The Old Schoolhouse Route 132, P.O. Box 183 Sharon, VT 05065 (802-763-2720)	Child's bedroom	Minimal materials used in construction. Wood is oak, which is under less environmental pressure. Pine and poplar, both sustainable domestic woods, are also used. Mattress is organic cotton and wool from undipped sheep.
Futon-style sofa, chair, and ottoman	The Futon Store 6969 E. Shea Scottsdale, AZ 85254 (602-596-1231)	Den	Made with organic wool and cotton fill. Upholstered in natural fibers dyed with vegetables. Wool is naturally fire retardant.
Modular sofa	August Incorporated P.O. Box 43 Centerville, OH 45459 (513-434-2520)	Living room	100 percent wool fabric (raising sheep for wool is considered a benign, sustainable activity). CFC-free foam cushioning.
Foam cushion for sofa, chair, and ottoman	E.R. Carpenter Company, Inc. P.O. Box 27205 Richmond, VA 23230 (804-359-0800)	Living room	CFC-free, polyurethane cushioning.
Chair and ottoman	Bernhardt Industries P.O.Box 740 Lenior, NC 28645 (704-758-9811)	Master bedroom	FoxFibre cotton covers filled with CFC-free foam
Steel chair frames	Grahl Industries, Inc. One Grahl Drive Coldwater, MI 49036 (517-279-8011)	Dining room	Requires minimum material to produce. Steel includes some recycled metal and is recyclable.
Fabric for dining chairs	Guilford of Maine 5300 Corporate Grove D, Suite 200 Grand Rapids, MI 49036 (800-648-9360)	Dining room	Synthetic fabric: production process uses less water, energy, and heavy metals than most synthetic fabrics.

Product	Manufacturer	Functional Area	Environmental Benefits
Furniture (cont.)			
Glass dining table and coffee table	Red River Studio Mark Tate, Carpenter 118 E. El Caminito Phoenix, AZ 85014 (602-870-1466)	Dining room and living room	Custom constructed using a base of sustainable veneers and Medite II from scrap materials left over during home's construction.
Axion task chair	Vitra 6560 Stonegate Drive Allentown, PA 18106 (215-391-9780)	Computer area	Uses minimal materials and virtually all parts are made of recycled and recyclable materials. Chair uses CFC-free recyclable polyurethane foam. Manufacturer has followed environmental principles in factory design.
Picto swivel chair and sled base chair	Wilkhahn, Inc. The Merchandise Mart Suite 1035 Chicago, IL 60645-1103 (312-527-1050)	Home office/guest bedroom	CFC-free polypropylene seat and backrest shells, joints, and linkages are mechanical and do not use glue or solder. Fabric cover is wool.
Stitz stools (cork seat)	Wilkhahn, Inc. The Merchandise Mart Suite 1035 Chicago, IL 60645-1103 (312-527-1050)	Kitchen	The seat is made from cork (generally obtained as a waste byproduct from the bottle-stopper industry). Cork is a highly sustainable material.
Stools (steel)	Kinetics, Inc. 110 Carrier Drive Rexdale, Ontario M9W 5R1 Canada (616-393-3000)	Kitchen	Steel frame is recyclable and may contain recycled material. The cover is made of worsted wool, a natural fabric that is durable and fire resistant.
Geoseat	Yemm & Hart RR 1, Box 173 Marquand, MO 63655-9610 (314-783-5434)	Child's bedroom, den	Made of compression-molded and extruded recycled postconsumer HDPE plastics. Metal fasteners are recyclable.
NOCH-BLOX Toy Box	Green Toy Store P. O. Box 982 Eureka, MT 59917 (800-532-0420)	Child's bedroom	Made of 100 percent postconsumer recycled plastics (HDPE).

Product	Manufacturer	Functional Area	Environmental Benefits
Special Construction			
Super II Pump and Motor, Micro-Clear DE Filter and Separation Tank	Hayward Pool Products, Inc. 2875 Pomona Blvd. Pomona, CA 91768	Pool pump, motor & filtration	Dual-speed pump cuts annual energy use by 30 percent. The DE filter allows 300 gallons of backwash water to re-enter the pool through a secondary filter thus saving water.
Challenger 3000 ionization system	Global Industrial Products, Inc. P.O. Box 12544 Scottsdale, AZ 85260-9998 (602-443-0481)	Pool sanitation system	Reduces reliance on chlorine. Purifies without the use of toxic chemicals.
Arneson Pool Vac	Arneson 2450 So. Watney Way Fairfield, CA 94533 (800-369-POOL)	Pool cleaning system	No need for energy-consuming booster pump.
Heliocol solar pool system with SunStar panels	Heliocol Arizona, Inc. 939 S. 48th St., #207 Tempe, AZ 85281 (602-967-6785)	Solar pool heating	Reduced energy costs over conventional electric or gas pool heating.
Save-T-Cover II	Cover Pools, Inc. 617 S. McClintock, #7 Tempe, AZ 85281 (602-829-0083)	Automatic pool cover	Provides safety factor. Extends life of pool materials, reduces evaporation of water and pool chemicals.
Pebble-Tec	Pebble Technology, Inc. 7950 East Acoma, Suite 105 Scottsdale, AZ 85260 (602-948-5058)	Pool surfacing material	More durable and limits the need for tile below the waterline. (Tile is very energy intensive to produce.)

Product	Manufacturer	Functional Area	Environmental Benefits
Mechanical/Plumbing			
Copper Cricket solar water heater	Sage Advance Corporation 1001 Bertelsen Road Eugene, OR 97402 (503-485-1947)	One of three water heaters used in home	Uses solar technology. Uses nontoxic solution in solar panels. Because of "geyser pumping action," requires no pumps or electricity.
E-Tech heat pump water heater, model WH-6	Crispaire Corporation 3570 American Drive Atlanta, GA 30341 (404-458-6643)	One of three water heaters used in home (garage display)	Uses an R-22 refrigerant. Can reduce the amount of energy required to heat water by as much as 60 percent. Provides cooling that can be directed to a home's ductwork.
Water heater tank	Marathon/Water Heater Innovations 3107 Sibley Memorial Highway Eagan, MN 55121 (612-688-8827)	Tank used to store hot water from each of the home's three water heaters	R-value of 25. CFC-free. Very durable.
Copper plumbing	Various manufacturers	Plumbing pipes and fittings	Made from up to 70 percent recycled materials.
Fluidizer low-flush toilet	Control Fluidics, Inc. 124 W. Putnam Ave. Greenwich, CT 06830 (203-661-5599)	Guest bath toilet	Lower water use (0.6 gals per flush) than current low-water consumption toilets. Hydraulic attrition-type flushing action.
Rialto Pressure Lite toilet	Kohler Company Kohler, WI 53044 (414-457-4441)	Master bath toilet	Low water consumption: 1.6 gals per flush. Pressure tank-type flushing action.
Briggs lavatory sinks	Briggs Industries, Inc. 4350 West Cypress Street, Suite 800 Cypress, FL 33607 (813-878-0178)	All lavatories	Possible recycled content. Recyclable.
Briggs Ultra-Conserver toilet	Briggs Industries, Inc. 4350 West Cypress Street, Suite 800 Cypress, FL 33607 (813-878-0178)	Children's bath toilet	Uses 1.5 gallons per flush. Gravity-type flushing action.

Product	Manufacturer	Functional Area	Environmental Benefits
Mechanical/Plumbing (cont.)			
Real Goods toilet lid sink	Real Goods 966 Mazzone Street Ukiah, CA 94582 (800-762-7325)	Children's bath (used with Briggs toilet)	Allows water to be used for hand washing prior to use for flushing.
Incredible Head shower head	Resources Conservation, Inc. Greenwich, CT 06836 (800-243-2862)	Master bath shower head	Exceeds EPA regulations of 2.25 gpm flow. On/off switch allows user to shut off water.
Chatham shower head	Chatham Brass Company 5 Olsen Ave. Edison, NJ 08820 (800-526-7553)	Children's bath shower head	Uses 2.25 gpm.
Alsons shower head	Alsons 525 E. Edna Place Covina, CA 91723 (818-966-1668)	Guest bath shower head	Low-flow shower head. Uses 2.0 gpm. Disabled-accessible wand-type head.
Flow-restricting aerator nozzles	Various manufacturers	Kitchen and bath faucets	Use lower flow rates to do same amount of rinsing.
Blanco stainless steel sink	Blanco America, Inc. 1001 Lower Landing Road, Suite 607 Blackwood, NJ 08012 (800-451-5782)	Kitchen sink	Made from recyclable, durable stainless steel. Built-in chute and container for compost waste.
AGWA Gray Water System (custom design)	AGWA Systems 801 S. Flower Street Burbank, CA 91502 (818-562-1449)	Gray water/rainwater reuse system	Uses wastewater that would have otherwise gone to treatment plant for landscape irrigation.
Galvanized metal ductwork	Various sheet metal manufacturers	All house and garage ducting	High recycled content and easily recyclable.
Trane Super Efficiency heat pump system	The Trane Company Unitary Products Group 6200 Troup Highway Tyler, TX 75711	Garage heating/cooling	Uses HCFC R-22, an intermediate replacement for CFCs. High SEER rating. Especially suited to saving energy in desert climates.

Product	Manufacturer	Functional Area	Environmental Benefits
Mechanical/Plumbing (cont.)			
Intertherm PowerMiser hot water integrated heat pump system	Nordyne 1801 Park Drive St. Louis, MO 63146-6911 (314-878-6200)	House heating/cooling, water heating	Uses HCFC R-22, a replacement for CFCs. Saves 80 percent energy over a typical water heater. Air conditioning function is 20 percent more efficient than federal standards.
Young Regulator Zonal Controls	Young Regulator Co. 20910 Miles Parkway Cleveland, OH 44128 (216-663-5646)	Zonal control system and zonal thermostats	Only areas occupied are heated or cooled.
Honeywell Chronotherm III programmable thermostats	Honeywell 1985 Douglas Drive North Golden Valley, MN 55422-3993	Programmable thermostat in home	Allows programmable control of heat pump so unit only operates at times when home is occupied, thus saving energy.
Panasonic central vacuum system	Panasonic 6550 Katella Avenue Cypress, CA 90630 (714-373-7200)	Central vacuum system	Improves indoor quality because it exhausts directly to outdoors. Uses no filters or bags.
Hunter ceiling fans	Hunter Ceiling Fans 2500 Frisco Avenue Memphis, TN 38114 (800-252-2112)	Ceiling fans	Reduces heating and cooling needs by de-stratifying air and increasing air movement in rooms of home.
Carrier Electronic Air Cleaner, Model 31KAX020	Carrier Corporation Syracuse, NY 13221 (800-CARRIER)	Air cleaner	Eliminates dust, pollen, and smoke from air inside home.
Panasonic ceiling-mounted ventilating fan	Panasonic 152 Technology Drive Irvine, CA 92714 (800-245-1068)	Bathroom ventilation	Quiet, less noise pollution than competitors. Low wattage.
Radon Passive Sub-Slab Depressurization System	U.S. Environmental Protection Agency Center for Environmental Research Information Cincinnati, OH 45268 (Publication #EPA/625/2-91/032)	Radon mitigation system	Installed for demonstration purposes. Perforated PVC pipe down the center length of the home draws radon and vents it through a vertical pipe through the roof. A fan can be added to move more air if necessary.

Product	Manufacturer	Functional Area	Environmental Benefits
Electrical			
Solarex Mega SX64 photovoltaic modules with AC converter	Solarex 630 Solarex Court Frederick, MD 21701 (301-698-4200)	Solar electricity generation	With three amperes of current at peak power, provides up to 20 percent of home's power needs. Offsets part of summer peak energy demand.
Energy-efficient lighting, compact fluorescent/halogen lamps	Various manufacturers	Lighting throughout home	Uses less than 50 percent of energy of typical home lighting.
LiteTouch 2000	LiteTouch 3550 South 700 West Salt Lake City, UT 84119 (801-268-8668)	Lighting control	Programmable system improves security and energy use and provides basic home automation functions.
Electric energy-dispensing system	Electric Vehicle Information Center Arizona Center 400 N. 5th Street Phoenix, AZ	Outside garage	Enables drivers of electric vehicles to power their vehicles' batteries. Electric cars are zero-emission vehicles.

List of Acronyms

ADEQ	Arizona Department of Environmental Quality
ADWR	Arizona Department of Water Resources
AIA	American Institute of Architects
APS	Arizona Public Service
CFC	Chlorofluorocarbons
EER	Energy efficiency rating
EPA	U.S. Environmental Protection Agency
ESH	Environmental Showcase Home
gpm	Gallons per minute
HCFC	Hydrochlorofluorocarbons
HDPE	High-density polyethylene
HVAC	Heating, ventilating, and air conditioning
kWh	Kilowatt-hour
LCA	Life cycle assessment
LSL	Laminated strand lumber
LVL	Laminated veneer lumber
OSB	Oriented strand board
PET	Polyethylene
PSL	Parallel strand lumber
PV	Photovoltaics
SEER	Seasonal energy efficiency ratings
VOC	Volatile organic compound

Index